JAN HASKINGS-WINNER / ROBERT MEWHINNEY

Passport to Civics

Pippin Publishing

Copyright © 2008 by Pippin Publishing Corporation
P.O. Box 242
Don Mills, Ontario
M3C 2S2

All rights reserved. No part of this publication may be reproduced or transmitted in any form or by any means, electronic, mechanical, or otherwise, including photocopying and recording, or stored in a retrieval system without permission in writing from the publisher.

Designed by John Zehethofer
Maps and charts by Christopher Johnson
Cartoons by Pat Cupples
Editorial consultants: Robin Bennett, John Herbst, Thomas Laver, Lela Lilko
Index: Kathryn O'Handley
Photo research: Kathryn O'Handley
Typeset by Kim Monteforte, WeMakeBooks.ca
Front cover photo composite: Getty Images / Photodisc, Ajay Photographics

Printed and bound in Canada by Friesens

We acknowledge the assistance of the OMDC Book Fund, an initiative of the Ontario Media Development Corporation.

Passport to Civics **by Jan Haskings-Winner and Robert Mewhinney**

ISBN 978-0-88751-125-7

10 9 8 7 6 5 4 3 2

Contents

Welcome to *Passport to Civics*   vii

1 Civics and You   1

TAP into Active Citizenship   1
Civics and Decision-Making   2
   The Three Levels of Decision-Making   2
      Case Study 1: The Man on the Bridge   4
      Case Study 2: The Unconscious Driver   4
Who Has the Power to Make Decisions?   4
   Power within Families   5
   Power within Schools   5
   Power within Communities   6
      Case Study 3: Traffic Light Debate   7
   Power within Nations   7
How Do Governments Make Decisions?   8
   What Is Democratic Decision-Making?   8
      Case Study 4: Same-Sex Marriage   9
      Case Study 5: Canadians in Afghanistan   10
   What Is Authoritarian Decision-Making?   10
      Case Study 6: Iraq   11
Decision-Making Power and Citizenship   12
   What Is a Citizen?   12
Beliefs and Values of Canadian Citizens   14
   Canada's Democratic Values   15
      Citizen in Action:
         Jean Vanier   15
      What Can You Do?
         Wear a Poppy, Thank a Veteran   16
Active Citizenship   18
      Citizen in Action:
         Corporal Ainsworth Dyer   19
      Case Study 7: "Love My Chinatown"   20
Chapter 1 Review   21
   Build Vocabulary and Understanding   21
   Think It Through   21
   Share Your Voice   21
   Show You Care   22
   Take Action Portfolio   22

2 Democracy in Canada   23

TAP into Active Citizenship   23
System of Government in Canada   24
   Canada's Constitutional Monarchy   24
   The Three Levels of Government   25
      Case Study 8: "New Deal for Cities and Communities"   26
      What Can You Do?
         Connect with Government   27
   The Structure of Government   28
      Citizen in Action:
         Michaëlle Jean   29
Government Leadership   31
   Political Parties in Canada   32
   The Election Process   33
      Citizen in Action:
         Mark Holland   35
      What Can You Do?
         Vote!   36
Types of Governments   37
   Majority Government   38
   Minority Government   38
      Case Study 9: Pass the Budget   39
   Coalition Government   40
Law-Making in Canada   41
   The Process of Turning Ideas into Laws   42
      Citizen in Action:
         James Bartleman   44
      Case Study 10: Ontario Helmet Law, 1995   45
      Case Study 11: Safe Drinking Water   45
      Case Study 12: Dog By-Law   46
   Who Else Has a Say in What Laws Are Passed?   46
      Case Study 13: First Nations Issues   48
Chapter 2 Review   49
   Build Vocabulary and Understanding   49
   Think It Through   49
   Share Your Voice   49
   Show You Care   50
   Take Action Portfolio   50

3 Rights and Responsibilities 51

TAP into Active Citizenship 52
The Constitution 53
   The *Canadian Charter of Rights and Freedoms* 54
      What Can You Do?
         Celebrate National Aboriginal Day 56
      Case Study 14: Wrong Place, Wrong Time 57
      Case Study 15: The Shoplifter 58
The Judicial System 59
   The Rule of Law 59
      Citizen in Action:
         Nelson Mandela 60
   Judges, Juries, and the Court System 61
Rights Abused, Restricted, and Upheld 64
      Case Study 16: Chinese Head Tax 65
      Case Study 17: The "Persons" Case 65
      Case Study 18: Internment of Japanese–Canadians 65
      Case Study 19: Treatment of People with Disabilities 66
      Case Study 20: Treatment of Aboriginal Peoples 66
      Case Study 21: The Keegstra Case 66
      What Can You Do?
         Stand Up to Hate 67
   Privacy Rights and You 68
      Citizen in Action:
         Ann Cavoukian 69
Canada's Youth Justice System 72
      Citizen in Action:
         Cindy Blackstock 73
      Citizens in Action:
         The Toronto Argonauts 76
The Responsibilities of Citizenship 77
      Citizen in Action:
         Tony Carella 78
      What Can You Do?
         Work to End Gender Violence 79
Chapter 3 Review 83
   Build Vocabulary and Understanding 83
   Think It Through 83
   Share Your Voice 83
   Show You Care 83
   Take Action Portfolio 84

4 Rise and Resolution of Civic Conflict 85

TAP into Active Citizenship 85
The Nature of Conflict 86
   Causes of Conflict 87
      Case Study 22: Fur 87
      Case Study 23: Forestry 88
      Case Study 24: Censorship 88
Conflict Resolution 89
   Strategies for Resolving Conflict 89
      What Can You Do?
         Volunteer 90
      Case Study 25: The People vs. McDonald's 92
      Case Study 26: Government Approach to Resolving Conflicts 93
      Citizen in Action:
         Richard Mewhinney 93
Conflicts with Government 94
   Aboriginal Peoples and Civic Conflict 95
      Case Study 27: Rail Line Blockade 99
      Citizens in Action:
         Inuit Circumpolar Council (ICC) 100
      Case Study 28: Negotiating on an Equal Footing 100
Environmental Conflicts 102
      Citizen in Action:
         Simon Jackson 102
      Case Study 29: Adams Mine 106
Chapter 4 Review 109
   Build Vocabulary and Understanding 109
   Think It Through 109
   Share Your Voice 110
   Show You Care 110
   Take Action Portfolio 110

5 Global Citizenship 111

TAP into Active Citizenship 111
Rights as Global Citizens 112
    The Universal Declaration of Human Rights 112
        Citizen in Action:
            Cardinal Paul-Émile Léger 114
        Citizen in Action:
            Ken Saro-Wiwa 114
Human Rights Violations Around the World 116
    The Islamic Republic of Iran 116
        Case Study 30: Zahra Kazemi 118
        Case Study 31: Republic of Zimbabwe 118
    Rwanda 119
        Citizen in Action:
            Stephen Lewis 122
    Child Soldiers 123
        Case Study 32: Children in Combat 124
        Citizen in Action:
            Craig Kielburger 126
Canada on the World Stage 127
    Canada's Role in International Affairs 127
        Citizen in Action:
            Jody Williams 128
    Canada's Response to Natural Disasters 130
    Tsunami in Southeast Asia 130
        Citizens in Action:
            International Federation of Red Cross and Red Crescent Societies 131
        Citizen in Action:
            Frank Stronach 132
    Earthquake in Pakistan 133
        Case Study 33: Response to Pakistan Earthquake 134
        What Can You Do?
            Join an NGO 134
Working Together for Change 135
    Citizens in Action:
        Doctors Without Borders/Engineers Without Borders 136
    Approaches to Active Citizenship 137
        Citizen in Action:
            Daniel Igali 138
The Well-Rounded Citizen 138

Chapter 5 Review 140
    Build Vocabulary and Understanding 140
    Think It Through 140
    Share Your Voice 140
    Show You Care 141
    Take Action Portfolio 141

Afterword 142
Glossary 143
Index 145
Acknowledgements 151

Welcome to *Passport to Civics*!

Your goal in this course is to learn what it means to be a Canadian citizen—what rights, privileges, and responsibilities you have as a member of this great nation.

Each chapter begins with an activity and a list of key ideas to help you focus on what you will learn in the pages that follow. "TAP into Active Citizenship" (together with the "Take Action Portfolio" section that ends each chapter) encourages you to apply what you are learning. By following this step-by-step guide, you will develop an action plan to help you in making a difference in an area of importance to you.

As you move into each chapter, you will see words in **bold letters** that may be unfamiliar to you. These words are defined in the margin as well as in the Glossary at the back of the book. You are encouraged to add these words to a personal dictionary, along with other words and phrases you learn as you work your way through this book.

The margin literacy links (words in blue in the margin) will help to enhance your understanding of text features, types of writing, graphic organizers, and so on.

Each chapter contains a number of other features as well.
- Case studies provide specific, real-world examples of the key ideas contained in the chapter.
- "Citizen in Action" profiles introduce you to Canadians who have made a difference at the local, national, or global level. Some of the people may be familiar to you, others you will be learning about for the first time. What they all have in common, though, is their commitment to making the world a better place to live.
- The feature titled "What Can You Do?" suggests ways you can become involved in active citizenship. You may find that you already contribute in some of the ways suggested.
- "Activate Your Thinking" activities give you the opportunity to make connections between what you will learn and what you already know or have experienced in your life.
- The "Apply Your Learning" activities help to reinforce what you have learned through your reading.
- Finally, the "Chapter Review" activities are structured to guide you in the following ways:
    - "Build Vocabulary and Understanding" identifies words you should know by the end of the chapter. Be sure to add these words to your personal dictionary if you haven't already done so during your work with the chapter.
    - "Think It Through" suggests ways to find out more information about the chapter's key ideas and how you can deepen your understanding of those ideas.

- "Share Your Voice" provides opportunities for you to communicate your learning in different ways to different audiences.
- "Show You Care" encourages you to reflect on how you feel about what you have learned in the chapter, and what steps you might consider taking as a result of your learning.
- "Take Action Portfolio" leads you step by step toward your final action plan.

By the end of this course, you will have the satisfaction of knowing that you have taken a big first step toward becoming an informed, purposeful, and active citizen of Canada and the world.

Jan Haskings-Winner
Robert Mewhinney

Toronto, March 2008

CHAPTER 1

Civics and You

Imagine you have to serve lunch to this group of people. The meal must be the same for each person, something that everybody can and would eat and enjoy. What are some issues you would need to consider and resolve? Share your ideas with the class. Try to reach an agreement on a possible meal choice. Discuss the difficulties of this process.

Key Ideas
In this chapter, you will learn about
- *democratic decision-making*
- *how decision-making power is distributed*
- *the beliefs and values of citizenship*

TAP into Active Citizenship

What problems or issues concern you? Do they relate to your school, your community, Canada, or another part of the world? Begin making a list of these concerns as you work your way through this and other chapters. Add to your list other issues that you learn about during this course. They might be issues that are covered in the news, or issues that other students find important.

Prepare a Take Action Portfolio (TAP). This could be a large file folder or an envelope. File the list and your ongoing notes in your Take Action Portfolio. This is an essential first step toward completing your culminating task.

Civics and Decision-Making

ACTIVATE YOUR THINKING

Create a chart in your notebook like the one below. For each statement, put a check mark under the appropriate heading. Compare your chart with that of a partner. Discuss two other decisions that you make entirely on your own. Add them to your chart.

Charts: charts help readers and audiences understand data at a glance, identify trends, and translate data into meaningful information.

Statement	I Decide	I Have Some Say	I Have No Say
Where I live			
When I go to bed			
When I wake up for school			
What school I attend			
What courses I take			
When I can legally drive			
What types of movies I can watch			
Who the next Prime Minister will be			
Where I work			
When garbage is collected in my community			

civics: the study of the rights and duties of citizenship

citizenship: the rights, duties, and responsibilities of a member of a state or nation

Civics is the study of the rights and duties of citizenship. **Citizenship** gives you the rights, duties, and responsibilities of a member of a state or nation. Civics has a lot to do with when, where, and how decisions that affect human needs are made, as well as by whom.

When you were much younger, your immediate family or caregivers made the decisions about your basic needs for food, clothing, and shelter. As you have matured, you have probably found that you are able to make more decisions about your personal needs, such as what to eat, what to wear, and who your friends are. At the same time, however, many of your needs involve decisions that have been made by institutions that exist outside your family, such as the school board and the government. The good news is that, as a citizen, you can play an important role in the decision-making process.

The Three Levels of Decision-Making

Decisions always involve choices and choices often have consequences (a result or outcome that follows). When you make a choice, you are making a decision. The decisions you make can be influenced by many things. For example:

- beliefs and **values** (personal or societal principles that govern a person's behaviour and choices)

values: personal or societal principles that govern a person's behaviour and choices

- how much money or time you have
- emotions
- goals
- needs
- personal safety and security
- likes and dislikes

What consequences will this cartoon character face, both good and bad, if he decides to break the computer?

Cartoons: cartoons use simple pictures that are stereotypes as short and effective ways of getting a message across to the reader. When you read a cartoon, ask:
- Who is the intended audience?
- What experiences, emotions, and attitudes is the cartoonist targeting?
- What visual symbol does the cartoonist use to represent the main idea?
- What is the cartoonist's intended overall meaning or message?

Some decisions are simple and require very little thought (like which toothpaste to use, or what to have for lunch). These are low-level decisions because they affect only you and have a short-term impact. Medium-level decisions are more difficult to make because they tend to affect not only you, but others as well (for example, what movie to rent when friends come over).

High-level decisions have a long-term impact. They can affect just you (such as choosing to take extra courses in math) or millions of people (such as choosing to drive a hybrid car to help the environment, the natural world that surrounds us). The more people the decision affects, the more complex the decision-making process becomes.

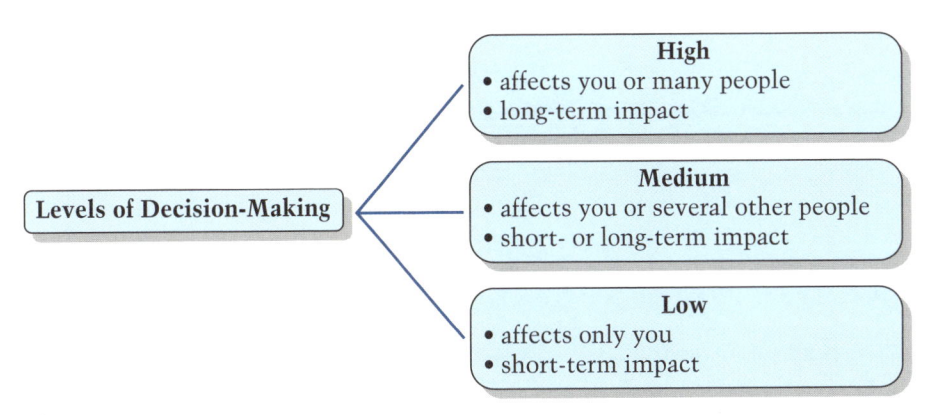

Levels of Decision-Making

High
- affects you or many people
- long-term impact

Medium
- affects you or several other people
- short- or long-term impact

Low
- affects only you
- short-term impact

Think about the range of possible choices facing the heroes in each of the following case studies. What thoughts might both women have had as they decided what to do? Put yourself in their position and jot down your ideas as you read.

Civics and You

Have you ever wondered what decision is best for you and your future? Making a decision can be difficult, especially when you are unsure of the outcome.

CASE STUDY 1: THE MAN ON THE BRIDGE

Several years ago, before special barriers were installed on Toronto's Bloor Street bridge, a bike courier saw a young man about to leap to his death. The courier had some big decisions to make and only seconds in which to make them. How could she save this man's life? She also had a delivery deadline. The documents she was carrying had to be delivered within the next five minutes to a location four blocks away.

At the risk of losing her job, she stopped and tried to convince the young man not to jump. After ten minutes had passed, the weeping man let her help him down. Moments later, emergency personnel arrived and took over. The courier told her story to the authorities and carried on, hoping that she would not be fired for missing her delivery deadline.

CASE STUDY 2: THE UNCONSCIOUS DRIVER

During the winter of 2005, a woman was driving with her young daughter on a busy Ontario highway. She noticed that the driver of a car in the passing lane was slumped over the wheel. She considered calling 911 on her cell phone, but she quickly realized that the fate of the driver, as well as that of other drivers, could not wait for outside help. She decided to speed up and place her car in front of the driverless automobile, risking her own life and that of her daughter. Using her own vehicle, she gradually brought the other vehicle to a stop just before it was about to go into the ditch. Within minutes, another motorist who knew first aid stopped. He was able to stabilize the unconscious driver until an ambulance reached the scene.

APPLY YOUR LEARNING

1. Do you think the woman in each case study made the correct decision? Why?
2. a) Think of a decision you have recently made. Would you consider it to be a low-, medium-, or high-level decision?
   b) Describe the process you went through to reach your final decision.

Who Has the Power to Make Decisions?

ACTIVATE YOUR THINKING

Create a list of words, or sketch some pictures or symbols, that represent what you think of when you hear the word power. *Organize your ideas in a mind map or a concept map.*

power: the ability to make things happen

Power is the ability to make things happen. By knowing where decision-making power rests within different organizations (groups of people that share common interests and purposes), it is easier to know where to get involved or with whom to talk if you have a question or a concern.

The distribution of power in families might be based on tradition, money, personality, or age. What determines the distribution of power in your family?

Power within Families

Every organization sets up a structure to determine how the power to make decisions will be distributed. Consider for a moment how power is distributed in your household or family. Is there one head of the household who has the power to make almost all of the big decisions? Or do two or more family members talk over the situation and decide together? Do all members of the household have an equal say, or do some family members have no say at all? What happens if there are differing opinions about a particular decision that has to be made? Does your family have a system or rules for settling disagreements?

The challenges that arise for a family making a decision are not unlike those that arise within large organizations. In both cases, those who hold the power to make a decision will consider the needs and interests of those who will be affected by the decision.

Power within Schools

One of the most important human needs is the ability to survive in society. This need is met mainly through the skills and education you acquire at school. At school, your teachers have the power to make decisions about the day-to-day activities that occur in the classroom. However, it is the administration (the people who manage and control an organization), made up of the principal and vice principal, which has the power to make larger decisions. These include the daily scheduling of classes, the types of events held in the school, how students are disciplined, and so on.

Many students discuss their future education plans with the school Guidance counsellor.

The provincial government has the power to decide which courses and how many of them you have to take to graduate. But you and your family have more say in the process than you may think. For example, you can choose the optional courses that will help you to achieve whatever long-term education or career goals you may have. Members of your family can join school councils, or can contact your school trustee or the Minister of Education if they believe that certain changes need to be made. If there is a serious concern about some aspect of your education, then a decision has to be made. The choice is either to remain silent and powerless, or to take action. Action will at least let the decision makers know that you are unhappy, and may even convince them to listen more closely or make a change.

This organizational chart shows the structure of decision-making in Ontario's education system.

Organizational chart: an organizational chart is a map or diagram that shows who is responsible for making decisions or how people or groups are related in an organization.

THE ONTARIO EDUCATION SYSTEM

Provincial Government (Ministry of Education)
↓
Local School Board Trustees
↓
Director of Education (and executive officers)
↓
School Principals
↓
Local School Community Councils
↓
Teachers
↓
Student Councils (represent students)

Power within Communities

In most Ontario communities, it is the members of the local government who hold the decision-making power. Yet there are many ways citizens can become directly involved in how their municipality (city or town) is run. They can sit on local committees and voice their opinions directly to city council. They can also make appointments at city hall to speak to their local representatives. In smaller communities, the councillors are often neighbours, active community members, or local businesspeople, making them readily available to the public. Since local government runs most of the services you rely on every day (such as garbage collection, public transit, and parks and recreation facilities), you are more likely to take action when you have a problem or a concern. Read Case Study 3 on page 7. List who was involved in the decision-making process.

If you want to take action on an issue in your community, it is helpful to get a local government official involved. Here, the mayor of Richmond Hill, Ontario, and local councillors join students to plant trees on Earth Day 2007.

6   *Passport to Civics*

CASE STUDY 3: TRAFFIC LIGHT DEBATE

The issue of replacing a crosswalk with a traffic light arose recently in a small Ontario town. Drivers were failing to stop at the flashing amber light above the crosswalk. The community raised the issue with municipal officials after several people were nearly hit.

City council debated the issue of installing a traffic light. Some councillors were concerned that local taxes would have to be increased to cover the extra cost. When they were unable to reach an agreement, they called an open community meeting. All interested residents were invited to voice their opinion. After much discussion, it was clear that the majority of residents felt safety was more important than the possible financial cost.

The local paper summarized the final decision with the headline, "Community gives green light to crosswalk safety."

Power within Nations

Decision-making power within most nations rests with those who run the governments of those nations. In many countries, such as Canada and the United States, the citizens choose who will run their governments. Regular elections allow citizens to change the leadership of their governments. This system gives the public a great deal of power in the decision-making process and in how their country is run.

In some countries, power is taken or held through the use or threat of force. The citizens of these nations have no say in who governs them, or in how they are governed. They are expected to obey their rulers without question. Countries such as North Korea, Cuba, China, and Burma (also known as Myanmar) follow this system of government.

Do not miss your opportunity to have a say in government. Vote in every election, whether it is at the federal, provincial, or municipal level.

APPLY YOUR LEARNING

1. Find an article in your local paper that deals with a decision affecting your community. Answer the questions that follow.
   a) Who had a say in the decision-making process?
   b) Who held the power to make the decision?
2. Do you think the decision that was reached was fair to everyone? Why or why not?

Civics and You

How Do Governments Make Decisions?

ACTIVATE YOUR THINKING

- *Brainstorm with a partner the similarities and differences in the way decisions are made in your home, your school, and your community.*
- *Brainstorm what you think of when you hear the word* authority. *Explain to a small group what your emotional reaction is to the word.*

Brainstorming: brainstorming starts a person or a group of people on their way to first ideas or subtopics. People often use brainstorming maps to record their initial ideas. Example:

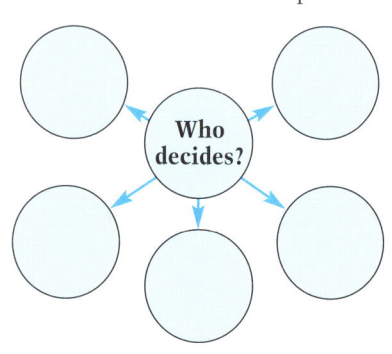

democracy: a form of government in which all people have equal political power and input

authoritarian: a system of government in which rulers expect complete obedience from those they rule

direct democracy: a form of government in which decisions are made by a direct vote of the citizens

indirect (representative) democracy: a form of government in which citizens elect representatives to make decisions on their behalf

One of your responsibilities as a citizen is to understand how your government works. When you know how government works, you can better understand the decisions it makes and how they affect you. You must then decide for yourself before the decision is made whether you agree with and support it, or disagree and oppose it. This is one reason why you study Civics.

Countries in which citizens can have a say in who runs their country and who makes decisions on their behalf are democratic. A **democracy** is a form of government in which all people have equal political power and input. Countries in which the citizens do not have any say in who runs their country or how it is run are authoritarian. Under an **authoritarian** system of government, unquestioning obedience to the ruling authority is expected.

What Is Democratic Decision-Making?

Democracy can take many forms. In a **direct democracy**, decisions are made by a direct vote of the citizens. Each person has a say in every issue, and each individual's vote has equal weight.

Canada is considered an **indirect** or **representative democracy**. People who are eligible to vote elect someone who then becomes a member of a legislative (law-making) body. In this law-making body, issues come forward that the members discuss. After the discussion, the members vote.

The elected members cast their vote on behalf of all the people they represent. Before the next election occurs, voters need to decide if they are satisfied with how they have been represented. If people don't like the way their representative has been voting, they can decide to vote for a different person, someone they believe will better represent their interests.

Characteristics of Democratic Decision-Making

When decisions are made democratically, there is usually more input from more individuals on what should be done. The beliefs and values of many groups will be expressed and considered in the process of making a decision. Ideally, the interests and beliefs of all people will be reflected in a final decision, but this is rarely ever possible. Our government has many factors to consider. For example:

Aboriginal peoples: a term used in a general way to refer to First Nations peoples, Métis, and Inuit. *First Nations* refers to the original inhabitants of what is now Canada.

culture: the beliefs, languages, customs, art, institutions characteristic of a particular community, people, or nation

- Canada was founded on the contributions of **Aboriginal peoples** (First Nations, Métis, and Inuit), the French, and the English. The term *First Nations* refers to the original inhabitants of what is now Canada.
- Canada continues to grow and prosper through the contributions of its large immigrant population, which includes many diverse cultures. (**Culture** is the beliefs, languages, customs, art, institutions, and so on that are characteristic of a particular community, people, or nation.)
- Canada is a bilingual country. Its two official languages are English and French.

As you can imagine, when the beliefs and values of all the different groups who make up Canada are considered, it is often quite difficult and time consuming to make decisions. The goal, therefore, is to provide the greatest benefit to the greatest number of people. This is called the **common good**. Recall the challenge at the beginning of this chapter. Did you consider the common good when you tried to come up with a meal that you could serve to such a diverse group of people?

common good: the interests of all people in a democratic society

When a vote is taken, the majority (more than half of the people in a group) determines the final decision. However, in Canada, there are many ways that the beliefs and values of the minority (fewer than half of the people in a group) are considered and voiced. Even when a decision is made, the opposition voice can continue to be expressed and heard.

As you read the following case studies, try to identify some of the characteristics of democratic decision-making.

CASE STUDY 4: SAME-SEX MARRIAGE

Same-sex marriage law passes 158–133

Wednesday, June 29, 2005 | 10:45 AM ET
CBC News

Newspaper articles: Most newspaper articles follow an inverted pyramid structure. Answers to the questions Who, What, When, Where, Why, and How are often provided in the first paragraph. Each paragraph that follows includes less and less important information. This way, if the article runs too long later paragraphs can be cut.

The Liberals' controversial same-sex marriage legislation has passed final reading in the House of Commons, sailing through in a 158–133 vote.

Supported by most members of the Liberals, the Bloc Québécois and the NDP, the legislation passed easily, making Canada only the third country in the world, after the Netherlands and Belgium, to officially recognize same-sex marriage.

The government has moved over the last few months to appease [soothe] critics both within Liberal ranks and among Canadians at large. Amendments were introduced to ensure no religious group or charitable organization would be forced to accept same-sex marriage. But in spite of those amendments some groups remain unconvinced.

Same-sex marriage remains one of the most difficult issues ever to confront Canadian politicians....

Civics and You 9

CASE STUDY 5: CANADIANS IN AFGHANISTAN

Tories urged to define Afghanistan commitment

Last Updated: Thursday, June 21, 2007 | 2:48 PM ET
CBC News

The federal government is facing more pressure to make a decision on the future of the Afghan mission as Canada mourns [shows grief for] the loss of three more soldiers.

NATO Secretary General Jaap de Hoop Scheffer will meet Thursday afternoon with Prime Minister Stephen Harper, Defence Minister Gordon O'Connor and Foreign Affairs Minister Peter MacKay in Ottawa to discuss the mission....

Harper's government has been under pressure in the House of Commons to define the length of Canada's commitment to the mission and make its intentions in Afghanistan clear.

Canada has committed troops to the war-torn country until February 2011. But its allies in southern Afghanistan are starting to ask questions about Canada's combat commitment and whether it will last beyond that deadline.

North Atlantic Treaty Organization (NATO): a group of 26 countries from North America and Europe committed to safeguarding the freedom and security of member countries by political and military methods

Acronyms: acronyms are abbreviations formed using the initial letters of words or word parts in a phrase or name. Acronyms are usually pronounced as the names of the individual letters (as in MP for **M**ember of **P**arliament, or OPP for **O**ntario **P**rovincial **P**olice), or as a word (as in NATO for **N**orth **A**tlantic **T**reaty **O**rganization).

APPLY YOUR LEARNING

1. Join a group of two other students. Discuss each of the following ideas for no more than two minutes. Try to cover a variety of beliefs and opinions. Think about the goal of providing for the common good. After each discussion, take a vote. Keep track of how many students in your group voted for and against each decision.
   - People under age 17 should have a 9:00 p.m. curfew (meaning they must remain indoors after that time) on weeknights.
   - The government should fund all faith-based schools.
   - Bicyclists should be licensed, just as drivers are.
   - Smokers should pay a fee for the medical care they receive.
   - Street racers who kill someone should serve a minimum 10-year jail term.
   - All schools will have a "uniform only" policy.
   - All Ontario high schools should install surveillance cameras.
2. What were some of the challenges of reaching a decision while at the same time considering the common good?

What Is Authoritarian Decision-Making?

Under an authoritarian government, opposition to the person or group in power is not allowed. The most important goal is to maintain the wealth and power of the ruler. When decisions need to be made, there is generally little or no attempt to seek input from groups who have different interests, or to gain the consent of the population. The common good is not considered. The power holders control the powerless, often through violence or terror. People or groups who oppose authoritarian rule are usually punished.

Characteristics of Authoritarian Decision-Making

In an authoritarian system of government, deciding what laws to pass and how to raise and spend money is very straightforward. Because opposition is not allowed, the government can, for the most part, do anything it wants, and do it very quickly. Such governments do not always follow a **constitution**, which is a set of rules and practices by which a country is run. Rather, those in power are free to make up whatever rules they wish. These rules benefit those in power first and foremost, rather than the citizens.

constitution: a set of rules and practices by which a country is run

Venn diagram: a Venn diagram is another type of visual organizer that is useful for comparing the similarities and differences between two or more sets of ideas or subjects. You can see an example of one to the right.

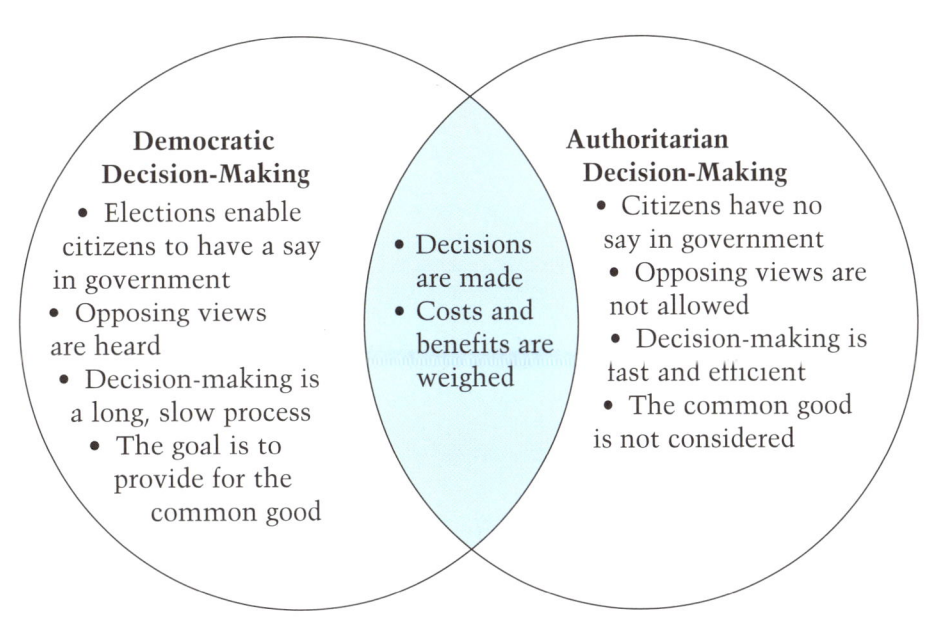

Democratic Decision-Making
- Elections enable citizens to have a say in government
- Opposing views are heard
- Decision-making is a long, slow process
- The goal is to provide for the common good

- Decisions are made
- Costs and benefits are weighed

Authoritarian Decision-Making
- Citizens have no say in government
- Opposing views are not allowed
- Decision-making is fast and efficient
- The common good is not considered

What characteristics of authoritarian rule can you identify in the following case study?

CASE STUDY 6: IRAQ

monarchy: rule by a king or queen

In 1958, the **monarchy** (rule by a king or queen) in Iraq was overthrown. The constitution was also thrown out. Between then and the Persian Gulf War in 1990, there were a number of unsuccessful attempts to create a new constitution. The final attempt gave total power to a single group who were members of the Baath Party.

Saddam Hussein, leader of the Baath Party, ruled Iraq from 1979 until he was overthrown in 2003 as a result of the invasion of Iraq led by the United States. As chair of the Revolutionary Command Council, Hussein passed over 1500 resolutions (laws) every year. Some of these laws changed the constitution or changed laws related to the security of the government and nation. Others changed laws concerning trade and taxes.

Among the many examples of brutality under Hussein's rule was the systematic killing of 148 Shia Muslims who opposed his authority. After his overthrow and arrest, he was found guilty of crimes against humanity and sentenced to death. He was hanged on December 30, 2006.

Creating a politically stable Iraq after 25 years of Saddam Hussein's rule has been a challenge. With no alternative system in place for making decisions, it has been difficult to determine what laws should be passed and how

A giant bronze statue of Saddam Hussein is removed from the Republican Palace in Baghdad in late 2003.

they should apply to the population. Iraq's situation is complicated by the fact that within its political boundaries live many different groups. In addition to the Sunni Muslim minority, of which Hussein was a member, there is the Shiite majority, as well as Kurds and Christians. A fair distribution of power between these groups has not yet been found even after an election was held in 2006.

APPLY YOUR LEARNING

1. Why would the actions of Saddam Hussein be more likely to occur in an authoritarian system than in a democratic system? Discuss your ideas with a partner.
2. Update the current Iraq situation using newspapers, magazine articles, documentaries, or the Internet.

Decision-Making Power and Citizenship

ACTIVATE YOUR THINKING

What ideas and images come to mind when you hear the word citizenship? *Write down as many of your ideas as possible.*

You now know that democracies are concerned with making the decisions that benefit the common good. But not every member of the population in a democratic country has equal decision-making power? In fact, only the citizens of a democracy have equal power.

What Is a Citizen?

A citizen is a member of a particular country. You are a citizen of Canada if you were born in Canada, or if you or your family were successful in your application for citizenship.

Canada's Citizenship Test

To apply for citizenship in Canada, you must be 18 years of age or older, or be part of a family group that is applying. You must legally be allowed to be in Canada, and have lived in this country for three of the last four years. You must speak either English or French, and you must pass a citizenship test. The test includes questions on topics such as the history and geography of Canada, elections, voting, the rights and responsibilities of citizenship, and so on.

SAMPLE CITIZENSHIP TEST: COULD YOU PASS?

1. How can you protect the environment?
   a) work near where you live, drive to work, take a taxi
   b) compost and recycle, conserve energy and water, walk or join a car pool
   c) pour paint down storm drains, leave taps running, leave lights on

2. What is Canada's system of government called?
   a) dictatorship   b) parliamentary government   c) military rule

3. What animal is an official symbol of Canada?
   a) deer   b) moose   c) beaver

4. Where are the Parliament Buildings located?
   a) Ottawa   b) Québec City   c) Toronto

5. Which province is the only officially bilingual province?
   a) New Brunswick   b) Québec   c) Ontario

6. What are the three main groups of Aboriginal Peoples?
   a) Cree, Haida, Inuit
   b) Inuit, First Nations, Métis
   c) Haida, Métis, Mi'kmaq

7. Which document made Confederation legal?
   a) British North America Act
   b) The Dominion Act
   c) The British Dominion Act

8. Who was the first Prime Minister of Canada?
   a) Louis St. Laurent
   b) Sir John A. Macdonald
   c) Pierre Elliott Trudeau

9. Which country is Canada's major trading partner?
   a) China   b) Britain   c) United States of America

10. Who is Canada's head of state?
    a) Prime Minister   b) Queen   c) Governor General

On July 1, 2007, 48 new citizens from across Canada took part in a special ceremony to celebrate the 60th anniversary of Canadian citizenship. Before 1947, people who lived in Canada were considered British subjects.

Answers: 1b, 2b, 3c, 4a, 5a, 6b, 7a, 8b, 9c, 10b.

Civics and You

When you pass the citizenship test and meet the other requirements, you will receive a *Notice to Appear to Take the Oath of Citizenship*. The document will tell you when and where the citizenship ceremony will take place. At the ceremony you will take the Oath of Citizenship along with others who have been asked to appear. When you have taken the oath (a formal, legally binding promise to do something) and signed it, you receive your Canadian Citizen Certificate. Many people bring family and friends to the ceremony, as becoming a citizen of a new country is one of the most important events in a person's life.

> **OATH OF CITIZENSHIP**
>
> *I swear (or affirm) that I will be faithful and bear true allegiance to Her Majesty Queen Elizabeth the Second, Queen of Canada, Her Heirs and Successors, and that I will faithfully observe the laws of Canada and fulfill my duties as a Canadian citizen.*

You might be wondering why the Oath of Citizenship is sworn to the Queen of Canada. You might also have wondered why the picture of the Queen is on stamps and coins. In Canada, the British monarch is considered the head of state (the main representative of a state or country) because of our British past.

APPLY YOUR LEARNING

1. a) Why do you think the citizenship ceremony is such an important event for a new Canadian?
   b) What other experiences in a person's life do you think would be similar?

Beliefs and Values of Canadian Citizens

ACTIVATE YOUR THINKING

Which of these ideas are beliefs and which are values? Compare your answer with that of a partner. Discuss the difference between beliefs and values.

friendship	*honesty*	*racial equality*
religious freedom	*kindness*	*democracy*
eco-consciousness	*courage*	*loyalty*

Beliefs and values guide our choices and actions. If you believe stealing is wrong, you will return your library books. If you value the environment, you will not litter. Beliefs and values define what a country considers important and what it expects from its citizens. We show our acceptance of and support for these beliefs and values when we follow the laws of the land and exercise our democratic freedom to vote.

Canada's Democratic Values

Citizenship and Immigration Canada describes our style of government as being "based on compromise and co-existence." We value our democracy and the spirit of co-operation that it promotes. We are willing to give up some of our individual wants and desires for the benefit of all Canadians.

CITIZEN IN ACTION

Jean Vanier

Jean Vanier began his career in the Canadian navy. He taught for a short while before becoming a chaplain in France in a centre for people with disabilities. In 1963, he founded L'Arche (translation *the arch*), a community for people with developmental disabilities (limited in their ability to learn and perform daily life skills). There are over 100 of these communities around the world. From its earliest beginnings, L'Arche was built on respect and the valuing of difference. Vanier believed it was not unreasonable to "dream of a world…where people, whatever their race, religion, culture, abilities or disabilities… can find a place and reveal their gifts."

Find out how you can get involved in volunteering or fundraising for L'Arche, or how you can become an assistant living in a L'Arche home. Share your findings with the class.

Jean Vanier

Canada's laws are based on our democratic values, which include:
- **Equality**—We respect everyone's rights. Governments must treat everyone with equal dignity and respect.
- **Freedom**—We enjoy basic freedoms, such as the freedom to think what we want, to speak out and express our own ideas without the fear of being punished, and to practise any religion.
- **Respect for cultural differences**—We try to understand and appreciate the cultures, customs, and traditions of all our fellow citizens, whether they were born in Canada or came here from another country.
- **Law and order**—We respect the process of democratic decision-making and support the rules and laws that result. We ensure that everyone is equal under the law, including our elected governments.

At a community reception in the village of Klukshu, Yukon, children perform a traditional dance.

- **Peace**—We are proud of our non-violent society and of our role as a nation that helps those in need around the world. We are particularly proud of the role we have played over the years as international peacekeepers.

The Peacekeeping Monument in Ottawa pays tribute to Canada's participation in international peacekeeping.

This veteran and the young sea cadets have all volunteered to serve their country. Do you think that it is easy or difficult to pass values like volunteering and self-sacrifice from one generation to another?

WHAT CAN YOU DO?

Wear a Poppy, Thank a Veteran

At the eleventh hour, on the eleventh day, of the eleventh month, Canada and many other countries around the world pause to remember those who have given their lives in war to protect our freedoms. November 11, known as Remembrance Day, is also a time to recognize the contributions and sacrifices of Canadians who helped bring peace to the world.

In the first half of the 20th century, over 1.5 million Canadians were called to defend peace and democracy across the world. More than 110 000 Canadians died serving in World War I, World War II, and the Korean War. Most joined the armed forces voluntarily. Today, Canadians still serve in peacekeeping missions around the world. Many have lost their lives trying to help others.

The poppy, a flower that grew on the battlefields of World War I, is a symbol of Remembrance Day. Veterans and members of the Royal Canadian Legion sell poppies to raise money for needy veterans and to raise public awareness of the beliefs and values connected with Remembrance Day.

In Ottawa, the Governor General, the Prime Minister, veterans, and others lay wreaths at the Canadian War Memorial on November 11. Similar ceremonies take place in parks, in schools, and at government buildings across the country. In 1999, the government of Ontario opened Highway 416, from Highway 401 to Ottawa, which it named

16   *Passport to Civics*

Canadian soldiers killed in Afghanistan are taken from CFB Trenton to the Centre for Forensic Sciences in Toronto before their bodies can be released to their families. Crowds often line bridges along the 172-km route named the Highway of Heroes, to pay tribute to these fallen soldiers as they pass by.

Veterans Memorial Highway. The Canadian government named 2005 The Year of the Veteran and the Royal Canadian Mint issued a special quarter in tribute. In August 2007, the Ontario government decided to rename a section of Highway 401 from Trenton to Toronto the Highway of Heroes to honour Canadian troops who fell in Afghanistan.

In Flanders Fields
by John McCrae

*In Flanders Fields the poppies blow
Between the crosses, row on row,
That mark our place; and in the sky
The larks, still bravely singing, fly
Scarce heard amid the guns below.*

*We are the Dead. Short days ago
We lived, felt dawn, saw sunset glow,
Loved, and were loved, and now we lie
In Flanders Fields.*

*Take up our quarrel with the foe:
To you from failing hands we throw
The torch; be yours to hold it high.
If ye break faith with us who die
We shall not sleep, though poppies grow
In Flanders fields.*

How does the marking of Remembrance Day reflect the democratic values and beliefs of Canadians? What more could we do?

APPLY YOUR LEARNING

1. How do you show your acceptance of, and support for, the democratic values listed on pages 15 and 16? Give an example from your day-to-day life for each one. For example, *I see my friends as individuals, not in terms of where they come from or what they look like.*
2. Which of the values listed on pages 15 and 16 is most important to you personally? Explain.
3. a) Describe the type of society we would live in if none of these values were upheld.
   b) Would you like to live in the society you described in part (a)? Why?

Civics and You

Active Citizenship

ACTIVATE YOUR THINKING

As a condition of graduating from high school, all Ontario students must provide 40 hours of volunteer service. Volunteering is just one example of active citizenship.

Brainstorm with your classmates all the ways someone could volunteer at the local, national, and global level.

Choose five of the ideas from the class list that you find most appealing. In what way does each of the five ideas reflect your beliefs and values?

As a citizen of Canada, you have the freedom to take direct action on issues that are important to you. In some cases, it is your duty as a citizen to take action. Active citizenship can take place at the local, national, or global level.

> local = your school or community
> national = the whole of Canada
> global = the world

Active citizens accept their responsibilities in the local, national, or global arenas. They might

- vote in every election
- contribute to society by participating in food or clothing drives, supporting community festivals, becoming involved in anti-discrimination activities, or taking action on a project of personal interest and importance
- share their hobbies, work, skills, culture, and values with others
- join a charitable or community organization, or other group that tries to improve the lives of others around the world
- show respect for the beliefs and values of others, and encourage their fellow citizens to do the same
- learn more about the freedoms and duties of citizenship

University of Guelph students register to vote.

Student volunteers with the Canadian Alliance for Development Initiatives and Projects (CADIP) work with children and help to build fences.

18   *Passport to Civics*

CITIZEN IN ACTION

Corporal Ainsworth Dyer

Corporal Ainsworth Dyer was born in Montréal of immigrant parents in 1977. While in high school, he helped start the school weightlifting club. He graduated from Eastdale Collegiate Institute in Toronto in 1997, and joined the Canadian army shortly afterward. He served with Canadian peacekeeping forces in Bosnia and Herzegovina in 2000 before heading to Afghanistan in 2002.

Since 2002, Canada has had an increasing military presence within the NATO forces in Afghanistan. Canadian forces are involved in Operation Enduring Freedom in support of the Afghan government against the Taliban and al-Qaeda. (The Taliban is a fundamentalist Sunni Muslim movement that ruled Afghanistan from 1996 to 2001. As of 2008, the Taliban was continuing to wage war against Afghanistan and NATO forces. Al-Qaeda is an international alliance of militant Sunni Muslim organizations.) Dyer was among the first Canadian soldiers to join the mission in Afghanistan. Sadly, he was one of four Canadians killed in what is termed a "friendly fire" incident. US Air Force pilots accidentally dropped a laser-guided bomb on Dyer and other Canadian soldiers who were participating in a training exercise.

Some of the memories Dyer's fellow soldiers had of him were shared at his funeral.

It was the type of character and personality he had that made him so enjoyable to work with. He always gave 110%. Our unit has lost a fine soldier and he will be sadly missed.
— *Warrant Officer Robitaille*

Ainsworth had a well-founded sense of right from wrong.... He never did things to gain acceptance from his peers if they conflicted with his ethics. Ainsworth was his own man; not a follower but a mature and thoughtful leader. One does not require rank or title to be a leader, just a well-founded character and charisma.
— *Corporal St-Laurent*

Since the death of Ainsworth Dyer in 2002, over 100 more Canadian soldiers have died in Afghanistan, including Captain Nichola Goddard, the first female Canadian soldier ever killed in combat. A person who dies while serving her or his country is always considered to be heroic, since life is a person's most valuable gift.

Find a recent article about a person whom you would consider to be a hero. File the article in your Take Action Portfolio under the title "A Citizen and a Hero." Give reasons for your selection in a short paragraph.

At his funeral, Dyer's sister Carolyn described him as "a beautiful person on the inside as much as on the outside. I can never be more honoured that he's my brother. I could never feel more proud, for he's my hero."

Captain Nichola Goddard was killed during a firefight in Afghanistan on May 17, 2006.

As you read the following case study, list the different ways that active citizenship is being demonstrated.

CASE STUDY 7: "LOVE MY CHINATOWN"

Diner takes on a litter hotspot

Huang Naili (STAFF REPORTER)

July 18, 2005
Toronto Star

Bill Lu often heard friends complaining about the filthy streets and the overpowering smells of downtown Chinatown. But it wasn't until he had dinner there last summer that the 40-year-old Mississauga resident decided to do something about it.

"The dinner itself was pretty good," Lu, a Chinese immigrant, said in Mandarin. "But outside, I was shocked by the litter and the stench from the overflowing trash cans. It's a big contrast with what we had enjoyed inside."

At first he decided to boycott [stay away from] Chinatown. But he changed his mind, because he realized "complaining…won't solve the problem."

He decided to wage a war against the dirty sidewalks of Chinatown…. He also wanted to set a good example of fulfilling a civic duty for his teenage daughter.

"I think a lot of us (immigrants) have to change the mentality [way of thinking] of being guests in a foreign country. We are hosts in our acquired country and we share the responsibility to make it clean and beautiful," he said.

He organized a group of volunteers, most of them Chinese immigrants, to clean the streets of Chinatown that were strewn with boxes, cigarette butts, food and food wrappings.

He named his campaign "Love My Chinatown" and more than 100 volunteers were mobilized to clean up the neighbourhood twice last year…

But ideally Lu would like local businesses to form an improvement association to monitor each other on community cleanliness. "If one store fails to keep its storefront clean, the association can give the owner a warning before he gets a ticket from the city," Lu said.

He believes the cleanup efforts will help create a win-win-win situation for the government, businesses and visitors who dine and shop in Chinatown.

Bill Lu, examining a typical assortment of rotting produce and cigarette butts at Spadina Avenue and Dundas Street West in Toronto. The area has many pedestrians, restaurants, and grocery stores.

Parentheses and brackets: printed text materials often use parentheses ( ) to mark for readers words, phrases, clauses, or sentences that function as explanations, translations, or comments. Square brackets [ ] used in quoted passages mark for readers text that has been added by someone other than the original author.

Expository or supported opinion paragraph: this type of paragraph uses researched facts and examples to support the writer's opinion about a topic. The paragraph starts with a *topic sentence* that clearly states the writer's opinion and previews the key points. The paragraph continues by identifying and explaining two or three *key points*, and ends with a *concluding sentence* that summarizes the writer's opinion.

APPLY YOUR LEARNING

1. a) Which of the activities on page 18 do you already do? Which activities do you see most students doing?
   b) What could schools or parents do to encourage you and your peers to participate more fully in some of these activities?
2. Write a paragraph that explains how Bill Lu became an active citizen. Follow these steps:
   • Start with a topic sentence that begins, "The main message that Bill Lu demonstrated was…."
   • Follow the topic sentence with two or three sentences that give examples to support your topic sentence (for example, why Bill Lu took on such a task).
   • End the paragraph with a concluding sentence that begins with something like, "In conclusion," or "To conclude," or "Therefore." Go on to explain your main idea about the topic.

CHAPTER 1 REVIEW

Build Vocabulary and Understanding

1. Refer to your personal dictionary. Select three words that help you understand the concept of civics.
2. Explain how each of the following concepts can be compared to one of the items in the box. (Hint: Describe the characteristics of the item first, and then determine how it is similar to the concept.)
   a) civics
   b) citizenship
   c) decision-making
   d) power
   e) values
   f) common good
   g) action
   h) duty
   i) culture
   j) constitution
   k) remembrance

For example, decision-making is like...
- a running shoe because by making a decision, you tie up loose ends
- a flower because it looks simple, but contains many parts
- a baseball cap because underneath is a lot of thinking
- a vacuum cleaner because it helps clean up messes

Think It Through

3. Select one event or person from this chapter that you see as representing the idea of civics. List all the reasons (evidence) you can find that support your choice.

Share Your Voice

4. Write a paragraph explaining why taking action in your community is important. Start your paragraph with your point of view (topic sentence), and provide at least three reasons for your point of view. Add a concluding sentence.
5. Select a concept from the list in question 2, above.
   - Create a visual to explain it to a newcomer to Canada, or
   - Prepare a brief oral presentation to explain to the newcomer the most important ideas behind the concept you have chosen.

Show You Care

6. a) Prepare an organizer on decision-making and power, showing where *you* fit in the process in your family, school, and community (for example, a club or team).
   b) List the people who have decision-making power in each of these categories. Include yourself.

Family	School	Community Organization/Group

   c) What can you do to gain more decision-making power in each group?

Take Action Portfolio

7. a) Brainstorm with a group of two or three other students issues that are important to you that require change in your community, in Canada, or in the world.
   b) Select an issue that you might like to investigate and identify it as a local, national, or global issue.
   c) Begin a log to record your progress and thoughts (see the sample that follows). Find other students in your class or community who might be interested in the same issue. You will find that sharing your learning on a topic of common interest will enrich your experience as an active citizen and help you to produce a better final product.

Date	Notes/Decisions	Level	Reflection and Next Steps
	Chapter 1: My selected issue of interest after brainstorming is...	☐ Local ☐ National ☐ Global	I chose this issue because...
		☐ Local ☐ National ☐ Global	

Passport to Civics

CHAPTER 2

Democracy in Canada

The English word *democracy* comes from the Ancient Greek word "demokratia," which means *rule by the people*. Study the illustration. If this is a picture intending to be a representation of democracy in Ancient Greece, how does democracy in Canada today differ? Who appear to be the decision makers in this particular system of government? How would you describe the role and attitude of the crowd watching the decision makers?

Key Ideas
In this chapter, you will learn about
- *Canada's system of government*
- *the election process*
- *how laws are made*
- *ways you can participate in the democratic process*

TAP into Active Citizenship

Newspapers and the Internet are filled with stories about issues of public concern, such as health care, the environment, gun violence, tuition fees, the military, and homelessness. As you work through this chapter, try to find two or more articles or websites related to the issue you chose at the end of Chapter 1. Keep track of these items in your Take Action Portfolio. You will need them to complete the next step in your culminating activity.

System of Government in Canada

ACTIVATE YOUR THINKING

How much direct involvement do you think governments have in your day-to-day life? Examine this street scene. Try to identify all the ways government might be linked to what you are seeing.

Government in Canada is based on a **federal system**. This means that decision-making power is divided between one central authority and several regional authorities. The central authority governs the country as a whole. The regional authorities are the governments of the provinces and territories that make up the federation (a group of various political units that have joined together to achieve common goals).

Canada's Constitutional Monarchy

When the plans to establish the country of Canada were being discussed, our leaders at the time were strongly influenced by the American Civil War that had just ended in the United States in 1865. They wanted a different type of federalism, one that would give the central government more control over the provinces. John A. Macdonald, who was Canada's first Prime Minister and a key player in the creation of the Dominion of Canada, argued for a **constitutional monarchy**. In this system, the nation's constitution and laws limit the powers of the monarch.

Almost everywhere you look, you can see examples of how government touches our lives.

federal system: governmental power is divided between one central authority and several regional authorities

constitutional monarchy: powers of the monarch are limited by the nation's constitution and laws

Representatives of the British North American colonies met at a series of conferences to draft the plans that would join them together in the Dominion of Canada. These men are often called the Fathers of Confederation. Whose interests might not be represented by these Fathers of Confederation?

24 *Passport to Civics*

The Three Levels of Government

On July 1, 1867, the British government passed a law that established Canada as an independent nation. Called the *British North America Act* (BNA Act), this law defined the powers that Canada's federal government (the central authority) and the provincial governments would have. Section 91 outlines the federal government's responsibilities, while Sections 92 and 93 outline the responsibilities of each of the provinces and territories.

Division of Responsibilities in Canada

Federal	Provincial/Territorial
Section 91 of the *BNA Act* • Aboriginal affairs and lands • banking • bankruptcy • census (information related to the country's population) and statistics • citizenship • criminal law (including trials, court procedure, and the federal prison system) • currency (money) and interest rates • employment insurance • fisheries • foreign affairs • immigration • marriage and divorce • national defence • navigation and shipping • postal service • patents and copyrights • public debt and property • taxation • trade and commerce (buying and selling of goods and services) internationally and between provinces • weights and measures	**Section 92 of the *BNA Act*** • administration of justice within the province/territory • civil law and civil rights • direct taxation within the province/territory • health care and hospitals • labour and trade unions • municipalities (cities, towns) and their governments and institutions • natural resources and the management of public land • property law • solemnization (ceremony) of marriage • welfare **Section 93 of the *BNA Act*** • education

The intention in 1867 was to give the responsibility over issues of national importance to the federal government. Issues at the local level, those that affected individual citizens more directly, were assigned to the provinces. This included overseeing municipal governments, which today manage such services as road and sidewalk maintenance, water and sewer systems, public libraries, and emergency services (fire, police, and ambulance). However, Canada in the 19th century was very different from Canada today. Some of what Canadians consider the most important government services simply did not exist in 1867; today these are provided by more than one level of government. Although rare, sometimes the different levels of government co-operate in providing services, especially those that affect a large percentage of the population (for example, health care, the environment, security, and transit).

In November 2006, Prime Minister of Canada Stephen Harper (centre), Ontario Premier Dalton McGuinty (left), and Mayor of Toronto David Miller (right) came together to support tough actions on gun crime. These men represent the three levels of government: federal (Harper), provincial (McGuinty), and municipal (Miller).

In 2005, the federal government made agreements with the provinces to provide a share of the gas tax to help municipalities. Much of the money provided through the "New Deal for Cities and Communities" goes toward public transit.

As you read the following case study, think about some of the reasons why it took so many years to reach this deal.

CASE STUDY 8: "NEW DEAL FOR CITIES AND COMMUNITIES"

Cities want share of federal gas tax

Last Updated: Sunday, February 17, 2002 | 10:24 PM ET
CBC News

Mayors from across the country are expected to ask for a share of federal gasoline taxes when they meet with high-profile cabinet ministers in Ottawa Monday.

Toronto city councillor Jack Layton, who chairs the Federation of Canadian Municipalities, said cities generate a lot of tax revenue for the federal and provincial governments, and that it's time they got some of it back.

"People feel if they're paying 13, almost 14 cents, to the federal government every time they pump a litre of gas, that at least some of that should be making its way back into moving people around in the cities," he said.

Layton said the mayors are hoping Environment Minister David Anderson will back their proposal to redirect a percentage of the federal gas tax to funding municipal transit. It would amount to three cents on every litre of gasoline....

In July 2005, municipal politicians from across Ontario celebrated the announcement of the federal government's agreement to provide a share of federal gas-tax funds to help cities and communities.

The "New Deal for Cities and Communities" is an example of all three levels of government working together in an area that is actually a municipal level of responsibility: public transit.

Canada's Three Levels of Government

Federal Government
- central authority
- decisions affect the entire country

Provincial/ Territorial Government
- regional authority
- decisions affect the province/ territory
- oversees municipal governments

Municipal Government
- local authority
- decisions affect cities/ towns

WHAT CAN YOU DO?

Connect with Government

Do you ever wonder how you can get involved in causes that are important to you? Asking questions is a good first step.
- What do you want to change?
- What, if anything, is being done to address this issue?
- What can you do on your own, and what will you need help with?
- Whom can you contact for help? What are your choices?

Writing a letter is often an effective way of getting involved. Letting your elected representatives know your views can help them make decisions that reflect your views. Be sure to do some homework before you write. Know the facts about the issue, as well as the point of view of the person to whom you are writing. Remember, elected representatives receive hundreds of letters, phone calls, and e-mails, so consider how to make your message stand out.

Here are some other tips for writing to elected officials:
- Identify yourself at the beginning of the letter.
- Be specific; state your concern or issue. Keep to the point.
- Briefly explain your viewpoint. If they already have a stated viewpoint on the issue, explain why you are for or against it.
- If you have a solution or an idea, share it, but keep it brief. Tell them what you want; don't expect them to guess.
- Request a reply and include your contact information: at a minimum your postal address, but also your home telephone number and e-mail address if you wish.
- Be polite and respectful.

---

123 Highbury Lane
My Town, Ontario K0Z 1K0

April 12, 2008

Ms. Franca Wardak
Councillor, Ward 6
City Hall, 1200 Centre Street South
My Town, Ontario K0Z 1K5

Dear Councillor Wardak:

My name is Sophie Tran and I am a Grade 10 student at Mount Carmel Secondary School. I am writing to voice my concern over the need for speed bumps on Elmwood Trail.

As you know, many motorists use Elmwood Trail as a shortcut between the city centre area and the highway, driving at speeds well above the posted limit. Three years ago, in response to the concerns of Elmwood Trail residents, the city installed "Slow Down, Think of Me" signs along the street to make drivers aware of the presence of children. This has done little to reform the behaviour of most motorists. The safety of Mount Carmel students and those who will be attending the newly built Elmwood Trail Public School is at risk. It is only a matter of time before someone is seriously injured or killed.

Installing speed bumps along Elmwood Trail would be a sensible, low-cost solution to the problem. Most of the residents I have spoken with are in favour of this solution.

I hope that as councillor for Ward 6, you will consider presenting this proposal to City Council at the next meeting. Please advise me of your decision regarding this issue.

Thank you for reading my letter and considering my suggestion.

Respectfully,

Sophie Tran

Sophie Tran

You can send your letter via Canada Post or e-mail. E-mail will arrive instantly and makes it easy to reply, but people tend to pay more attention when someone takes the time to actually mail a letter.

In addition to writing letters, here are some other ways to influence the government's decision-making process:
- Develop a local network of people who are willing to write letters in support of the same cause. The more messages elected representatives get about the same issue, the more likely they will be to act.
- Submit a petition.
- Attend community council meetings and make presentations, when possible.
- Apply to become a member of a citizen-appointed board.
- Vote in every election as soon as you are eligible to do so.

Identify an issue of importance to you. Find out which level of government deals with issues in this area, and then write a letter to the appropriate elected representative.

The Structure of Government

Our federal government is divided into three separate branches: the legislative, the executive, and the judiciary. Each branch of government has very distinct powers and responsibilities.

The legislative branch consists of the **House of Commons** (also referred to as **parliament**) and the **Senate**. The legislative branch of government is the main decision-making body in Canada. Members of the House of Commons (called *Members of Parliament* or *MPs*) are elected by the citizens of Canada. Members of the Senate are appointed by the prime minister.

The executive branch consists of the governor general, who represents the monarch, the government leaders (prime minister and cabinet), and the administration (civil service). The political party that receives the most votes usually forms the government. The leader of this political party is the prime minister, who then appoints members to the cabinet. Cabinet ministers make major policy decisions and head departments, such as defence, foreign affairs, immigration, health, and so on. Usually, prime ministers will select members of their own political party from different parts of the country to serve as cabinet ministers. Civil servants, who work to bring policy ideas into reality, staff each department.

The third branch of government is the judiciary. This is the legal system of courts. Judges in Canada are appointed by the government. The highest court in the country is the Supreme Court of Canada.

House of Commons (parliament): place where elected members of parliament (MPs) meet to discuss, debate, and vote on laws that the government wants to pass

Senate: forms the legislative branch of government, along with parliament; consists of appointed representatives who review and approve or request changes to laws proposed by parliament

THE THREE BRANCHES OF THE FEDERAL GOVERNMENT

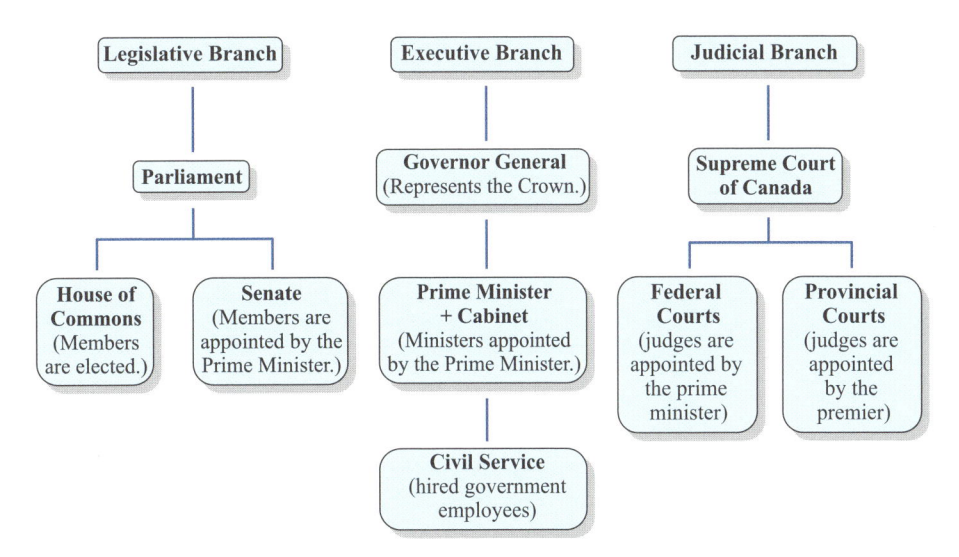

```
Legislative Branch          Executive Branch           Judicial Branch
       |                           |                          |
   Parliament              Governor General            Supreme Court
                        (Represents the Crown.)          of Canada
       |                           |                          |
   ┌───┴───┐                       |                      ┌───┴───┐
House of   Senate           Prime Minister            Federal    Provincial
Commons  (Members are          + Cabinet              Courts      Courts
(Members  appointed by the  (Ministers appointed    (judges are  (judges are
are       Prime Minister.)  by the Prime Minister.) appointed by appointed
elected.)                                           the prime    by the
                                   |                minister)    premier)
                              Civil Service
                           (hired government
                               employees)
```

At the provincial level, there is only one legislative house in all provinces but Québec. The executive branch consists of a lieutenant governor, who is the crown's representative, the provincial premier and his or her cabinet, and the civil service. The provinces have supreme courts, which are lower than the Supreme Court of Canada.

The governor general at the federal level and the lieutenant governor at the provincial level are appointed by the British monarch on the advice of the Prime Minister of Canada.

CITIZEN IN ACTION

Michaëlle Jean

Today's Canada has more voices than before—each calling out to be heard, to be respected and to be understood. The diversity of our landscape, people and cultural backgrounds gives us a sense of community in Canada.

— *Michaëlle Jean, August 4, 2005*

Michaëlle Jean and her family came to Canada as refugees in the late 1960s after fleeing the violent dictatorship of their native Haiti. She studied languages at university in Canada and abroad, and went on to become a journalist with Radio Canada and the CBC. Michaëlle Jean has been involved in helping women and children in abusive relationships, and has been very active in aid organizations for immigrant women and families. She has won many honours and awards for her journalistic achievements and social activism. In 2005, Michaëlle Jean was appointed as the 27th Governor General of Canada. She is one of only three women in Canada's history to hold this post.

Governor General Michaëlle Jean awards the Medal of Bravery to Daniel Harold Peacock, 15, of Rimbey, Alberta, in June 2007. Peacock risked his life to save a friend from drowning.

The role of governor general is somewhat controversial. Some Canadians believe that since we are an independent country we do not need a representative of the British monarch and the position should be eliminated. Others like the tradition of the role, and appreciate the duties performed by the governor general. What is your opinion? Read the list of duties that the governor general performs and then decide for yourself.

throne speech: a speech written by the governing party, which outlines their plans for leading the government

Role of Canada's Governor General

Duties as the Crown's Representative	Ceremonial Duties
• ensures there is always a prime minister in office • reads the **throne speech**, which outlines the intentions of the governing party for the upcoming parliamentary session • acts on the advice of the prime minister and cabinet ministers to give royal assent (agreement) to bills (laws) passed in the Senate and House of Commons • signs state documents • supervises the oath taken by the prime minister, chief justice, and cabinet ministers to uphold the constitution of Canada and to be loyal servants of the Crown • dissolves or suspends (prorogues) Parliament so that an election can be held • serves for a five-year term, which can be extended to seven years	• promotes national identity and unity within Canada by participating in many events, such as the celebration of Canada Day and Remembrance Day • travels to foreign countries at the request of the prime minister to promote and represent Canada • welcomes world leaders and receives foreign dignitaries in Canada • presents a variety of honours and medals, such as the Order of Canada and the Caring Canadian Award, to deserving Canadians

Which types of experiences and qualifications do you believe are the most relevant for the role of governor general?

APPLY YOUR LEARNING

1. a) Make a final list of all the activities you did or will do today.
   b) Put a check mark beside those activities that you think may have involved the government. For example, do you know who provides the power that runs your electronic appliances?
   c) Identify which level of government you think provided the service. Discuss your ideas with the class.

2. A 2003 survey done by the Centre for Research and Information on Canada found that 56 percent of Canadians thought the federal government had too much power. In the same survey, 32 percent of Canadians felt provincial governments needed more power, while 45 percent thought more power should be given to local governments. Why might so many Canadians want their provincial and municipal governments to have more power?

Surveys: surveys are a good tool to use when you want to get a general understanding of people's opinions on certain issues. Responses often reveal patterns or trends. This information can be used to develop recommendations, suggestions, or further questions.

3. Find one newspaper article related to each of the federal, provincial, and municipal levels of government. Place them in your Take Action Portfolio under the title "Canada's Three Levels of Government in Action."

Government Leadership

ACTIVATE YOUR THINKING

Have you or someone you know ever been chosen to lead a team, club, or event? What qualifications (for example, experience, personality, skills and abilities) were needed to become the leader? Write down as many ideas as you can.

political parties: voluntary associations of citizens who hold similar beliefs, values, and ideas on issues related to government

Political parties lead federal and provincial/territorial governments in Canada. **Political parties** are voluntary associations of citizens who hold similar beliefs, values, and ideas on issues related to government. In our democratic, federal system, Canadian citizens choose the political parties that will lead the federal and provincial/territorial governments. At the municipal level, citizens choose a candidate, not a political party, to lead their local government.

Stephen Harper, leader of the Conservative Party of Canada, was sworn in as Canada's 22nd Prime Minister on February 6, 2006.

Democracy in Canada   31

Political Parties in Canada

In June, 2007, there were fifteen political parties registered with Elections Canada. In March 2007, there were nine political parties registered with Elections Ontario. By registering, a political party can have candidates to represent it in elections. Almost all candidates in federal and provincial/territorial elections represent one of Canada's political parties. Occasionally, an election will have independent candidates (people who are not connected to any political party).

Some political parties are large and have a great deal of public support. They are considered mainstream parties because they represent widely accepted beliefs, values, and ideas. Smaller political parties, which tend to represent less popular or more extreme views, are considered fringe parties.

You may have heard or read about some of the political parties listed below. Which of them do you think are mainstream? Why?

Logos: logos are symbols that organizations use to make them easily recognizable to the public. Political parties give careful thought to the design of their logos.

FEDERAL POLITICAL PARTIES AND THEIR LOGOS

Conservative Party of Canada

Bloc Québécois

Christian Heritage Party of Canada

First Peoples National Party of Canada

Green Party of Canada

Communist Party of Canada

New Democratic Party

Marijuana Party

Libertarian Party of Canada

Liberal Party of Canada

The main goal of any political party is to lead the government. That's where you come in. Citizens have a very important role to play in deciding which political party leads their government. As with most democracies, there are very clear rules about how governments are elected.

32 *Passport to Civics*

The Election Process

Federal and provincial/territorial elections in Canada must be held every five years, but they can be held more frequently, depending on the circumstances. Sometimes, an election is called early because the political party in power is confident it can win again. At other times, the government is forced to hold an election when it no longer has the support of the majority of the elected representatives in government. Traditionally, however, elections are held at four-year intervals.

Municipal government elections are also held every four years. Candidates for mayor (or reeve in smaller towns and villages), city council, and local school boards must have the support of a specific number of residents of the city, town, or community where they are running. They must also pay a small fee to run. Municipal election candidates are not officially connected to a political party.

The federal election process begins when the prime minister visits the governor general and requests permission for an election to be called. At the provincial/territorial level, it is the premier who asks the lieutenant governor to call an election. In 2007, the *Canada Elections Act* was amended to state that an election must be held on the third Monday of October every four years after the previous election, but the Governor General still has the power to dissolve parliament on the advice of the Prime Minister.

Electoral Districts

Once an election date is set, political party candidates begin the process of convincing voters in their area to elect them as their representative in government. But the sheer size of Canada makes it impossible to have a representative in the federal government for every city, town, or community. For this reason, the country is divided into electoral districts. Electoral districts, which are also known as *ridings* or *constituencies*, cover a large geographical area. Currently, Canada is divided into 308 electoral districts. A Member of Parliament (MP) represents each one of these electoral districts. Ontario is divided into 107 electoral districts, and each one is represented by a Member of Provincial Parliament (MPP). When you vote on election day, you are helping to decide who will sit in government on your behalf and represent the needs and interests of the riding.

Election Campaigns

Campaigning is the process by which candidates try to persuade potential voters to elect them. They do this by
- advertising (lawn signs, posters, newsletters, and phone calls)
- debating issues with other candidates in public forums
- taking advantage of free air time on radio and television to get their message out
- knocking on doors
- making speeches
- being very visible and accessible to the citizens in their riding

Her Excellency the Right Honourable Michaëlle Jean, the 27th Governor General of Canada, met with the Right Honourable Paul Martin, former Prime Minister of Canada, on Tuesday, November 29, 2005. During their discussion, the Prime Minister asked the Governor General to dissolve Parliament, to which she agreed. This is the first step in the election process.

Liberal MP Ruby Dhalla campaigns door to door in her riding of Brampton–Springdale during the 2006 federal election. Why do you think it is important for political candidates to campaign door to door during an election?

Democracy in Canada 33

Political party leaders at both the federal and provincial/territorial levels extend their campaigning beyond the boundaries of their individual ridings. During federal election campaigns, party leaders crisscross the entire country. They try to meet voters in as many electoral districts as possible. This helps to generate support for the local candidate and to raise awareness of their party's plans and policies, or *platform*, for governing should they win the election.

The minimum length of a general election campaign at the federal level is 36 days. In Ontario, the election period is approximately five weeks; however, because general election dates in Ontario are fixed, many candidates start laying the groundwork for an election well in advance of that five-week period.

Unless specifically disqualified under the *Canada Elections Act* (sections 3, 4, and 65), a person need only be qualified to vote (be at least 18 years old on election day and hold Canadian citizenship) to run as a candidate.

Candidates from all local parties are invited to debate and speak to voters at an all-candidates' meeting.

Voters' List

Elections Canada is an independent organization responsible for ensuring federal elections are carried out properly and fairly. It keeps a database of all qualified, registered voters. Elections Ontario is the agency that oversees elections in this province and maintains the voters' list. If you are not a registered voter, you can still be added to the voters' list if you meet the criteria (are 18 and a Canadian citizen) and can provide suitable identification to an official on election day.

But it wasn't always this easy to vote in Canada. Certain restrictions were applied to different groups of people at different times in Canada's history. Women did not get the full right to vote until 1918. Chinese-Canadians could not vote until 1947. People who did not own property could not vote until 1948. Inuit received the right to vote in 1950, but First Nations peoples living on reserves had to wait until 1960. In 1970, the voting age changed from 21 to 18, with the 1972 federal election being the first in which 18-year-olds voted.

CITIZEN IN ACTION

Mark Holland

A proposal to lower the voting age from 18 to 16 was put forward by Liberal MP Mark Holland in 2005. Holland is a young MP himself, who was first elected in 2004 to represent the Ontario riding of Ajax–Pickering. He was re-elected in 2006.

Although Holland and his supporters agree that the minimum age to run as a candidate should remain at 18, they believe that lowering the minimum voting age to 16 would reverse voter apathy (lack of interest) in young people. Since many government decisions affect citizens under the age of 18, the argument follows that they should be given a voice in who makes those decisions. For example, 16-year-olds can work and pay taxes, get a driver's licence, and be tried in court as an adult. At age 17, they can join the military. At age 14, they can join a political party.

Arguments against lowering the voting age include the belief that young people are not mature enough to understand the issues, and cannot appreciate the importance of voting and the impact it will have on their future.

There seem to be more arguments for than against lowering the voting age, but it is far from becoming a reality.

Hold an informal debate in your class on the issue of whether the voting age should be lowered to age 16. Think of reasons why politicians would want to keep the voting age at 18.

Election Day

On election day, all eligible voters are free to go to their local polling station and cast their vote (or ballot). Polling stations are buildings within a riding that have been designated by election officials as the place you must go to vote. They are usually located in public buildings, such as schools and community centres, and are open for a fixed number of hours on the day of the election. Voters unable to attend a polling station on election day have the option of voting in an advance poll. Ballots cast in an advance poll are not counted until after the polls close on election day.

The election officials who staff each polling station ensure voting procedures are carried out according to the law. These workers, many of whom are volunteers, check that you are eligible to vote, provide you with your ballot, show you how to complete the ballot, and direct you to the polling booth where you mark your ballot. They must also

Mark Holland, MP, Ajax–Pickering

Christine Jairamingh (centre) and Eryn Fitzgerald (right), tried unsuccessfully to challenge the voting age in court. Here, the young women are addressing students at a high school in Edmonton, Alberta.

Debates: debates are an effective way of exploring opposing sides of an issue. Participants form two teams. Each team presents facts and information to support their point of view and to highlight weaknesses in the other team's position on the issue. Arguments are logical and designed to persuade an audience.
  A well-planned and organized debate is an effective way to resolve an issue or reach a decision.

Democracy in Canada 35

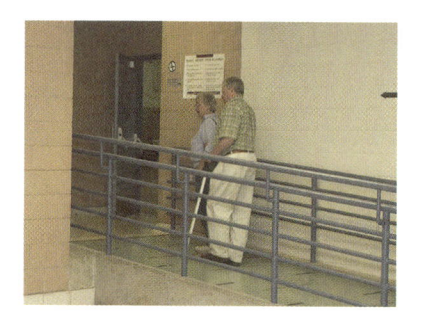

All polling stations must be accessible for people with disabilities.

Marking a ballot:
- The ballot will list the names of all the candidates in your riding. A circle will be beside each name. The candidates' political parties will NOT be on the ballot.
- The District Returning Officer (DRO) will explain what to do with the ballot. It is the DRO's job to answer any questions you have about the ballot.
- A screen will be set up so you can vote in private. Take your ballot there. No one should see how you vote. Unfold your ballot. Mark an "X" in the circle beside the name of the person you want to elect.
- After you mark your "X," refold your ballot. Hand it to the DRO, who will put your ballot in the ballot box. You are finished voting.

ensure that you have free and easy access to the polling station and are given the opportunity to cast your ballot in private.

At the end of the day when the polls close, the ballots are counted and the results are passed on to a returning officer, who is in charge of the election process for that riding. The returning officers, in turn, provide the results to the chief electoral officer, who eventually files an official report on the outcome of the election.

WHAT CAN YOU DO?

Vote!

A very important way to participate as an active citizen in your democracy is to vote. Think about whom you want to represent your views about how your city, your province/territory, or your country is run. Although very few high school students are of legal voting age, Student Vote elections give them the opportunity to participate in the process.

Just like the actual election, students attend polling stations within participating schools and vote. The ballots are the same as those all eligible voters in the riding receive. Students mark their ballot and place it in the box. The votes are counted, often by students in civics classes, and reported back to Student Vote. Results are released after the close of polls—just like the official election—and printed in newspapers following election day.

Study the following table of results from the 2006 federal election. What similarities and differences can you see between the Student Vote results and the final election results?

Party	Student Votes %	Seats	Canada Votes %	Seats
Conservatives	31.29	127	36.27	124
Liberals	21.95	53	30.23	103
Bloc Québécois	1.59	34	10.48	51
NDP	23.07	62	17.48	29
Independent	1.28	1	0.52	1
Green	16.74	7	n/a	n/a
Other*	3.7	0	5.02	0

*Represents 11 different political parties across Canada.

Voter apathy, especially among young adults, is a major concern in every election. In 2004, the overall rate of participation (those who could vote and did) was just over 60 percent, the lowest rate ever in a Canadian federal election. But the worst turnout was among voters

Whether you mark your ballot with an X or use an electronic voting machine, one of your most important civic duties is to vote!

aged 18 to 30. Elections Canada tried hard to get them to vote, but only 38 percent of them did (although this was higher than the 25 percent who voted in the previous election). Within the 18 to 30 group, only 25 percent of those under age 25 cast their ballots. Compare that to the 80 percent of those over 65 who voted! This means that people over 65 had more of a voice in the federal government that was elected in 2004 than young adults. Do you think issues important to 65-year-olds are the same as issues important to 18-year-olds? Think about this the next time an election rolls around. What issues would motivate you to vote? A law requiring students to stay in school until age 18? Setting a higher minimum wage for students? Identify at least three other issues that are important to you.

Working with a partner, list reasons why young people do not vote. Join another pair group and discuss possible solutions to the poor participation of young people in elections.

APPLY YOUR LEARNING

1. a) Research to find out three facts about your electoral district and your Member of Parliament.
   b) Identify one thing that you find interesting, one thing that you learned, and one thing that you would still like to discover.
2. If an election is currently happening (federal, provincial/territorial, or municipal), find an article that refers to the major issues and place it in your Take Action Portfolio under a title that clearly identifies the election. For example, "November 2006 Municipal Election in [name of your community]."
3. Which step in the election process do you think is most important to
   a) a political candidate?   c) an elections official?
   b) a political party leader?   d) a Canadian citizen?

Types of Governments

ACTIVATE YOUR THINKING

Based on what you have read, heard, or seen on the news recently, what type of government do we have today in Ontario? In Canada? How do you know? Share your answer with a partner.

The party winning the greatest number of ridings in an election normally forms the government. The leader of the party that wins a federal election becomes prime minister. The leader of the party winning a provincial election becomes premier. By forming the government, the party has the power to bring forward the policies that it feels are most important. Before the next election, the leading party will try to pass as many of its policies into law as possible.

"Isn't that the real genius of democracy?...The VOTERS are ultimately to blame."

Explain why, in a democracy, "The voters are ultimately to blame."

Democracy in Canada 37

In Canada, there are three types of governments that might be formed after an election: majority, minority, and coalition.

Majority Government

The success of the government in turning the policies it thinks are important into laws depends on having the support of a majority of the members of parliament. It is much easier for the government to gain this support if a majority of MPs (or MPPs at the provincial level) are members of the governing political party. In other words, if more than half of the ridings in an election vote for a candidate from the same political party, a **majority government** results.

When a party forms a majority government it has a great deal of power to pass laws that it believes are important for the country. Some would say that majority governments are more stable because when MPs are required to vote on major government initiatives, such as laws and budget estimates, they tend to vote the way their political party expects them to vote. If most of the members of the House of Commons are from the governing political party, the laws and budgets the government puts forward get passed quite easily. Others argue that such governments give too much power to one party.

majority government: when one party has enough members in the House of Commons to outnumber the members of all other parties

When a government holds a majority, the other parties in Parliament have limited power.

Minority Government

A **minority government** is one in which the governing party does not control a majority of the seats in Parliament. This type of government obtains the power to lead by gaining the support of opposition party members. These are elected representatives from other political parties, as well as independent members (those who ran as independent candidates and have no connection to a political party). The support of an opposition party or member is usually given on the condition that the governing party makes certain changes to legislation

minority government: when the governing party controls fewer seats in the House of Commons than all other parties combined and must rely on MPs from other parties to support its legislation

38   Passport to Civics

that the supporting party would like. This support does not involve the party becoming part of the government's ministerial team, and support may not extend to the government's entire legislative program. A minority government must work continually to gain support beyond its own party members for every piece of legislation.

Minority governments are not necessarily unstable or short lived if they can come to an agreement with another party and win its support, especially on key laws that have to be passed. Such a situation can make governments more responsive to the views of other parliamentary members, which can result in a more open and flexible approach to governance.

The main concern of a minority government is that the support keeping it in office can be withdrawn at any time. When a key piece of legislation such as a budget is defeated in a vote, it is presumed that parliament, the voice of the people, no longer has confidence in the leadership ability of the government. This is called a **vote of non-confidence**, and it means that the government must resign or must ask the governor general to dissolve parliament so that an election can be called, or to prorogue it (suspend it temporarily).

Read the following case study. Try to identify three challenges a minority government might face.

vote of non-confidence: a successful vote of non-confidence forces the government to resign and an election to be called. If a government budget or proposed law having to do with spending or raising money is ever defeated, it is considered a vote of non-confidence.

prorogue: to discontinue parliament without formally ending the session

CASE STUDY 9: PASS THE BUDGET

Maiden Tory budget wins Commons approval

Updated Wed. May 10, 2006 11:26 PM ET
CTV.ca News Staff

The minority Conservative government survived its first major confidence test Wednesday night as its maiden budget passed easily in a House of Commons vote.

Despite opposition from the Liberals and NDP, the Tories' fiscal agenda was virtually assured approval because of the endorsement of the separatist Bloc Québécois.

The budget passed easily in a vote of 175 to 113. Former Prime Minister Paul Martin, the federal finance minister between 1993 and 2002, made a relatively rare appearance to vote against the budget with his fellow Liberals.

Conservative MPs paused briefly in their voting to give a standing ovation to Finance Minister Jim Flaherty, who first introduced the budget to the House of Commons on May 2.

Despite the budget winning approval in principle, the battle over its details will likely continue with legislation to implement specific measures still to come.

Those measures will need to pass not only the Commons but also the Liberal-dominated Senate later this year.

Prime Minister Stephen Harper stands in the House of Commons to vote in favour of his party's budget.

Political Parties in Opposition

A key component of any democratic system is ensuring the government remains accountable to the people who elected them. One way this is achieved is through opposition parties. People who are elected to the House of Commons or a provincial legislature who are not

Democracy in Canada   39

members of the party that forms the government are referred to as the *Opposition*. Their role is either to suggest ways that government policies could be improved, or to voice their disapproval of policies that they believe are not in the best interests of the voters who support their party. Opposition members try to make sure that voters know what the government is trying to do and make them aware of alternative points of view.

Usually the party with the second highest number of votes forms the Official Opposition, and its leader is recognized as the Leader of the Official Opposition.

There are financial and political advantages to gaining this position. In the House of Commons, the Leader of the Official Opposition has more contacts with the media (journalists and news broadcasters) than the leaders of other opposition parties, and also has more time during **question period** to ask the government questions. Question period is that part of the day during the sitting of the House of Commons when Members of Parliament in opposition (or MPPs in the provincial legislatures) can ask the government questions. Also, in a political sense, the opposition party presents itself to Canadians as the alternative choice of government at the time of the next election. The amount of influence that an opposition party leader has is partly determined by the size of the government majority. If, instead of a majority, an election results in a minority government, the opposition leader will have a much greater influence.

Coalition Government

A coalition government consists of two (and occasionally more than two) political parties that work together to gain a majority position in government or to increase their influence in Parliament. The coalition parties may indicate before an election that they intend to work together if they win office, or coalition agreements may be formed after the election when it is clear that no single party has a majority of seats. In 1985, Ontario had a coalition government, led by Liberal leader David Peterson allied with the NDP.

When a coalition government is formed it means that, at least temporarily, the government will continue to operate without the need to call another election. In times of crisis, such as war or national emergency, parties might agree to create a coalition to ensure that the government can make decisions about serious issues with less delay. Such agreements rarely last for an extended period, and opposition parties are often reluctant to make such arrangements. The reason for this is that often voters in the next election will think that there is no point voting for the smaller party's candidates because they will just join the government anyway. This is a political reality that is understood by all political leaders.

The role of the opposition is to ask the prime minister and his or her cabinet ministers probing questions or questions that force them to explain the actions of the government. Michael Ignatieff was elected Liberal opposition leader in May 2009.

question period: part of the day during the sitting of the House of Commons (or legislative assembly at the provincial level) when opposition members can ask the government questions

coalition government: a government consisting of two or more political parties, neither of which has a clear majority of the seats in parliament. These parties unite to form the government, dividing the cabinet positions between them.

APPLY YOUR LEARNING

1. Review the 2006 federal election results in the table that follows.

Party	Seats	Vote Share
CON	124	36.27%
LIB	103	30.23%
BQ	51	10.48%
NDP	29	17.48%
IND	1	.52%
OTH	0	5.02%

   a) Which party won the election? How do you know?
   b) What type of government is this?
   c) Who can work together to defeat the government? What will happen if they do this?

2. a) Compare the share of vote with the percentage share of seats shown in the table. For example, you need to figure out whether 124 seats is 36.27% of 308.
   b) Which parties might be concerned about the share of the vote, and why?

3. Create a chart in your notebook like the one below. Compare your completed chart with that of a partner. Add any new ideas you learn from your partner to your chart.

Type of Government	Characteristics	Advantages	Disadvantages
Majority			
Minority			
Coalition			

Law-Making in Canada

ACTIVATE YOUR THINKING

Brainstorm with a partner some of the laws of which you are already aware. What are the possible reasons for each of the laws on your list?

One of the main responsibilities of any government is to pass laws that not only ensure the smooth running of the country or province/territory, but that also reflect the changing needs and interests of Canadian citizens.

Democracy in Canada 41

The Process of Turning Ideas into Laws

All laws begin as ideas. An elected member of parliament suggests that a law should be made. It starts out as a bill. A bill is a legal document, one that usually contains many pages and sections. This proposed law is usually introduced by a cabinet minister and sponsored by the government. It deals with the interests of a citizen, a group, an institution, or a community. There are also private members' bills, which can by introduced by any member of parliament. Liberal MP Mark Holland's proposal to lower the voting age to 16 is an example of a private members' bill.

An MP sitting in the House of Commons has many duties, including asking or responding to questions and voting on bills.

For a bill to become law at the federal level, it must go through a specific process. This process includes several steps or stages, first in the House of Commons, and then in the Senate. If it passes successfully through each stage, as a final step it goes to the governor general, who signs it into law.

Often, because there are so many voices and opinions to be heard and considered, a bill has to be changed before it is passed into law. In this way, the concerns and rights of minorities and special interest groups are taken into account. Once a bill has been passed into law in a democratic state, *all* people who are living in that state must obey it.

The flow chart that follows explains each step in the process of passing a bill into law. After you read the chart, discuss with a partner some of the advantages of there being so many steps before a bill becomes a law in Canada. What are some of the disadvantages?

Flow chart: a flow chart is a picture that describes the process of steps followed to accomplish a project or a task

HOW A BILL BECOMES A LAW

The cabinet minister responsible for the government department initiating the policy prepares the bill. The Department of Justice reviews the bill to ensure it doesn't conflict with other laws.

HOUSE OF COMMONS

First Reading
The bill is read in the House of Commons and members of parliament vote on it. The details of the bill are not discussed at this point.

Second Reading
MPs discuss the principle (main idea) of the bill. They are allowed to speak only during the debate. After the debate, another vote is taken.

Committee
MPs on the appropriate parliamentary committee study the bill clause by clause (each paragraph). MPs can suggest amendments (changes) as well. They then present their report to the House of Commons.

Third Reading
The bill is debated again. This debate is usually brief, as most of the concerns have already been addressed.

SENATE

First Reading
After the bill passes the third reading in the House of Commons, the bill is read in the Senate and the senators vote on it. Again, there is no discussion.

Second Reading
Senators discuss the principle of the bill.

Committee
Senators on the appropriate Senate committee study the bill clause by clause. They make changes, if necessary.

Third Reading
The bill is read in the Senate and a vote is taken.

The bill is given royal assent with the signature of the Governor General. It is then an Act of Parliament.

Queen's Park in Toronto houses Ontario's provincial legislature. The premier and members of provincial parliament conduct government business in this building.

In Ontario, laws are passed in a similar way, but there is no Senate or Governor General. Instead, it is the Lieutenant Governor who signs bills into law after third reading in the legislature.

Democracy in Canada 43

The Honourable James K. Bartleman served as Canada's ambassador to numerous countries, including Cuba and Israel. He was also High Commissioner to Cyprus, South Africa, and Australia before he was appointed Lieutenant Governor of Ontario in 2002.

Well-known TV personality David Onley became Ontario's 28th Lieutenant Governor in September 2007, replacing James Bartleman. Stricken with polio as a child, Onley is partially paralyzed from the neck down. He is actively involved in the Canadian Foundation for Physically Disabled Persons and the Ontario March of Dimes. How has the cartoonist promoted Onley's appointment as being very positive?

Autobiography: an autobiography is an account of a person's life written by that person. The writing is often vivid and personal in nature.

CITIZEN IN ACTION

James Bartleman

James Bartleman was born in Orillia, Ontario, to a Scottish–Canadian father and an Ojibwa mother. Growing up, he experienced both poverty and discrimination because of his Aboriginal background. However, a man for whom he worked heard that Bartleman was a good student and offered to pay for his university education. This break led to a very successful 35-year career in the Canadian Foreign Service.

Bartleman overcame many obstacles on his road to success, which sparked his passion to help others. Being a member of the Mjnikaning First Nation has also given him first-hand knowledge of the challenges many Aboriginal peoples living in Canada face.

When Bartleman became Ontario's 27th Lieutenant Governor in March 2002, he identified three areas of focus for his term in office:
- to encourage Aboriginal communities, especially the young people in those communities, to develop their literacy skills
- to support initiatives that fight racism and discrimination; and
- to raise awareness of, and support for, people struggling with mental illness.

As you can see, there is a strong connection between James Bartleman's personal life experience and the goals he set for himself as lieutenant governor. His first book, *Out of Muskoka*, won an award in 2003 as the best book on multicultural history in the previous three years. He donated all his royalties (the money he received for writing the book) to the scholarship fund of the National Aboriginal Achievement Foundation. The royalties from his second book, *On Six Continents*, pay for public lectures on topics concerning mental health.

In 2004, Bartleman launched a campaign for the donation of books to First Nations communities. This was an opportunity for many people to become active citizens. Students at Westmount Public School in London, Ontario, met the challenge of the lieutenant governor's book program by donating thousands of books to the cause.

In 2005, yet another initiative was launched, when 85 public schools throughout Ontario were twinned with a First Nations school to promote literacy among Aboriginal youth. The goal was to build bridges between Aboriginal and non-Aboriginal student communities. Public school students became pen pals with Aboriginal students. Participating schools conduct annual drives to continue the donation of books and musical instruments for Aboriginal children, as well as hosting an Aboriginal awareness week in their schools each June.

Write a brief autobiography. Identify at least two personal experiences that you have had that could become your focus as an active citizen.

Passing laws at the municipal level follows a process similar to that at the provincial and federal levels. City or regional councillors, or other elected representatives, bring forward issues and debate the merits of by-laws. However, because councillors are not associated with a specific political party, it is sometimes difficult to predict how a vote will go. A councillor who generally votes on one side with a certain group of like-minded councillors may vote against her or his usual allies if it is in the best interests of the voters in his or her ward. On the plus side, this is a sign that those elected at the municipal level are more closely linked to the needs and concerns of the people who elect them. On the negative side, it is sometimes difficult for an elected mayor to get the council to vote for the policies or promises for which she or he was elected.

As you read the following case studies, record in your notebook answers to the following questions:
- Which level of government is involved?
- Why was the law passed?
- Who started the law (private member or government minister)?
- Who signed the law? Why?

The Rainy River Valley Safety Authority, a community group in northwest Ontario, gave out coupons for free ice cream cones to children who obeyed the bike helmet law.

CASE STUDY 10: ONTARIO HELMET LAW, 1995

If you ride a bicycle on a road or sidewalk in Ontario and are under the age of 18, you must wear an approved helmet. This law was passed in 1995. Parents can be charged if they knowingly allow their children under 16 to ride a bicycle without a helmet.

The law was passed after London MPP Dianne Cunningham introduced a private member's bill in response to the injury of a friend's child, as well as requests from community groups, such as the injury prevention community group. The bill was first introduced in 1990 and reintroduced in 1991, with the support of the NDP who formed the government at the time. After much debate and consultation with community groups, such as those working to promote safer cycling, Bill 124 was passed into law in July 1993. It came into effect on October 1, 1995.

There have been some attempts to require skateboarders and scooter riders to wear helmets, but no law has been passed.

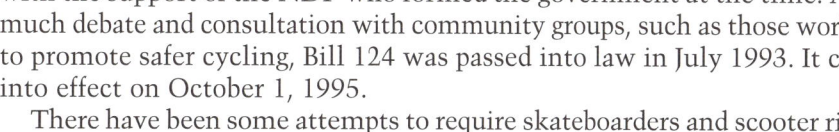

CASE STUDY 11: SAFE DRINKING WATER

In 2000, seven people in the town of Walkerton died from drinking infected water. As a result of these deaths, and the far-reaching public inquiry into them, the provincial government introduced several significant new laws intended to protect drinking water. The new laws include the Safe Drinking Water Act, the Sustainable Water and Sewage Systems Act, and the Nutrient Management Act. Justice O'Connor, who led the inquiry into the deaths at Walkerton, also recommended that legislation to protect sources of drinking water be enacted in Ontario. This legislation is currently being developed by two government-appointed committees.

Democracy in Canada

City Hall—Waterloo, Ontario

CASE STUDY 12: DOG BY-LAW

THE CITY OF Waterloo

CITY OF WATERLOO
BY-LAW NO. 91-101
CONSOLIDATION

BY-LAW TO PROHIBIT THE RUNNING AT LARGE OF DOGS IN THE CITY OF WATERLOO, FOR IMPOSING A LICENSE FEE ON THE OWNERS OF DOGS, FOR REGULATING THE DISPOSAL OF DOGS FOUND RUNNING AT LARGE IN THE SAID CITY AND FOR OTHER MATTERS RELATING TO DOGS.

WHEREAS the Municipal Council of The Corporation of the City of Waterloo deems it desirable to prohibit the running of dogs at large in the City and otherwise providing for the seizing, impounding and killing of dogs running at large and for selling dogs so impounded as hereinafter set forth and for licensing and regulating the owners of dogs in the said City.

PASSED this 12th day of August, 1991.

(SIGNED) B.TURNBULL
MAYOR

(SIGNED) R.C. KEELING
CLERK

interest groups: organizations that try to influence the government to make changes in laws or policies that will benefit their members or support a specific cause

Students from Calgary Christian School present Lee Richardson, MP for Calgary Centre, with a petition asking the Canadian government to look into atrocities in Uganda. Lee Richardson later presented the petition in the House of Commons.

Who Else Has a Say in What Laws Are Passed?

There are many ways you can influence the law-making process in Canada. You can become an elected representative at the provincial or federal level of government. You can join a political party and influence its policies. You can be informed and vote in elections for people who are concerned about the same issues as you. You can volunteer to work on an election campaign, where you can be in close contact with potential decision makers. You can also join an **interest group**. Interest groups (sometimes called *pressure groups*) are organizations with a specific focus. They try to lobby (influence in various ways) the government to make changes in laws or policies that will benefit their members.

Lobbying is one way individual citizens can voice their opinion to government officials about government policy actions. It is basically an information-sharing process. There are two types of lobbying: casual lobbying and professional lobbying.

Casual Lobbying

As an individual citizen you can lobby the government in a number of ways. You can meet with members of the government directly. Writing a letter expressing your point of view is another method. An interest group can organize and send e-mails, faxes, postcards, or letters to cabinet ministers or members of parliament. The more correspondence elected representatives receive, the more notice they will take of your concerns.

Professional Lobbying

Groups of people who decide to work together to lobby the government about issues of concern to them often hire full-time staff and fundraise to make money to pay the staff. There are many professional lobby groups, from those representing Aboriginal peoples, manufacturing sectors, and grain growers, to tobacco companies, firearms associations, and marketing boards. You may already be familiar with some of the issues they address, such as urban affairs, education, seniors, the environment, fisheries, and health care.

The government of Canada has established policies and laws for paid lobbyists. These rules exist to guard against powerful lobby groups having too much influence over politicians and the decisions they make.

> The Lobbyists' Code of Conduct is based on four principles, which are stated in the *Lobbyists Registration Act*:
> - Free and open access to government is an important matter of public interest;
> - Lobbying public office holders is a legitimate [lawful] activity;
> - It is desirable that public office holders and the public be able to know who is attempting to influence government; and,
> - A system for the registration of paid lobbyists should not impede [stand in the way of] free and open access to government.

The Media

A final method of influencing government is through the media (newspapers, magazines, radio, and television broadcasts that reach a very large audience). All interest groups attempt to gain the attention of the media, as the media provide information on different issues and analyses of the issues themselves. Major media institutions are corporations, so they also have an editorial policy that identifies the point of view that they are trying to promote.

Look at the news headline and short clipping in the case study that follows. What method of lobbying is being used? What evidence do you have?

Democracy in Canada

CASE STUDY 13: FIRST NATIONS ISSUES

Assembly of First Nations National Chief Calls on Premiers to Work with First Nations to "Close the Gap" in Quality of Life During Council of the Federation Discussions

August 9, 2005

Today in Calgary, Assembly of First Nations National Chief Phil Fontaine called on provincial and territorial leaders to address First Nations issues as part of an effort to close the gap in the quality of life between First Nations and the rest of Canada. He issued the call at a meeting with provincial and territorial premiers and national Aboriginal leaders prior to the Council of the Federation meeting in Banff, Alberta.

APPLY YOUR LEARNING

1. a) Take turns with a partner explaining how a bill becomes a law in Ontario and in Canada.
   b) Why is there a difference?
2. a) Brainstorm with a small group ideas for laws that you would like to see changed or passed.
   b) Choose one law and work together to draft the wording of it.
   c) Explain why you think your proposal should be accepted.
   d) To which level of government would you submit your proposal?
3. Which of the case studies in this section have the greatest impact on you personally? Explain.
4. Which of the principles in the Lobbyists' Code of Conduct do you think is most important in a democracy?

CHAPTER 2 REVIEW

Build Vocabulary and Understanding

1. Take turns with a partner using each of the following words in a sentence. Be sure to add the following words to your personal dictionary.
   - a) democracy
   - b) federal
   - c) municipal
   - d) election
   - e) vote
   - f) Parliament
   - g) House of Commons
   - h) Senate
   - i) bill
   - j) political party
   - k) majority government
   - l) civil service
   - m) lobbying

Think It Through

2. a) Together with a small group, brainstorm as many services as you can think of that are provided by the three levels of government.
   b) Identify the level of government responsible for each of the services you listed in part (a).
   c) Record the top three services provided by the three levels. Rank them in order of importance. Use the following to help you organize the services.

Rank	Service Provided	Level of Government	Explanation of Ranking

T-charts, fish diagrams, spider maps: these visual organizers are useful for comparing ideas, information, or resources. T-charts are used to compare differences, details, and points of view (pro/con, for/against). Fish diagrams are often used for listing more than one cause for a historical event, and spider maps can help to organize the relationships between events or ideas.

3. Create a T-chart of pros and cons on the following issues:
   - corporate funding in exchange for advertising in schools
   - legalizing marijuana
   - lowering the drinking age to 18 for those in the military
   - lowering the voting age to 16
   - limiting the contents of vending machines in schools to healthy foods only

Share Your Voice

4. Choose four words from question 1. Prepare to role-play a situation with one or two classmates that demonstrates how these words are related.

5. Prepare a visual representation that shows your understanding of three of the words in the first question. You can use stick people if you like.

Show You Care

6. Select a law that has been passed, or one that you believe should be passed. Explain how it relates to your life. Provide examples from your own family or personal experience, showing how it will be important in the future. You can write this as a paragraph or, if you prefer, you can express it orally.

Take Action Portfolio

7. a) Find two articles or websites on your topic. Take notes to summarize the issue using a graphic organizer such as a spider map or a fish-scale diagram (see samples). Ask a peer to check that you have clearly identified the key concepts. File the original items as well as your notes in your Take Action Portfolio.

SPIDER MAP

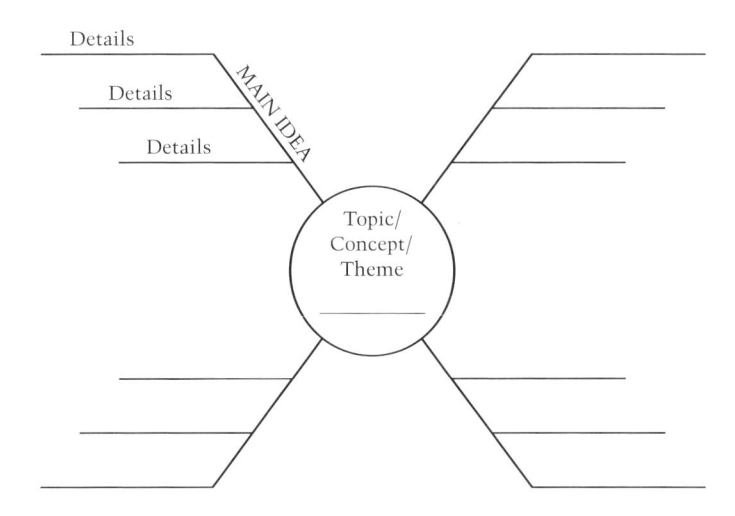

FISH-SCALE DIAGRAM

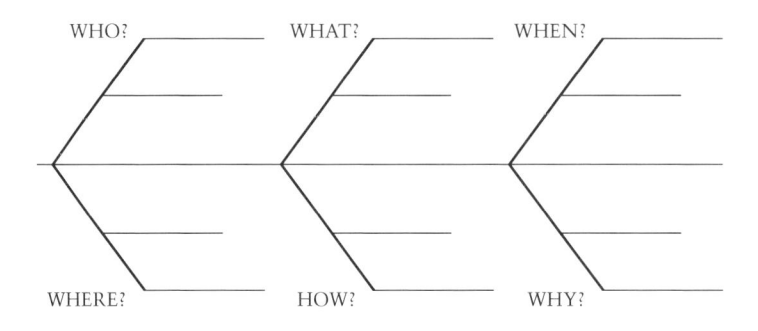

b) Find or create a map that shows where this issue takes place (where in your community or province, in Canada, or in the world). File the map in your Take Action Portfolio.

c) Update the log you began in Chapter 1, summarizing your progress on your issue to date. If you have decided to change your choice of topic, provide an explanation and identify who you might be able to work with on this issue.

CHAPTER 3

Rights and Responsibilities

Passenger with infectious disease boards airplane in defiance of doctor's orders

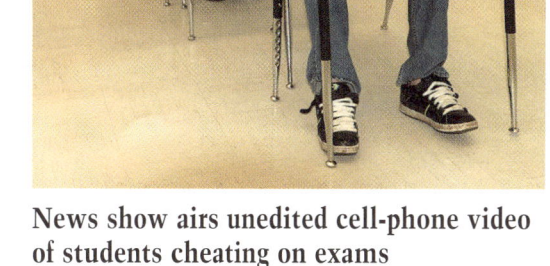

News show airs unedited cell-phone video of students cheating on exams

Passport denied to Canadian citizen with past ties to terrorist group

Read the headlines on pages 51 and 52. Using your own definition of a right and a responsibility, identify what rights and responsibilities are involved in each situation. For example, people have a *responsibility* not to break copyright laws by downloading music without payment. The recording industry has the *right* to receive payment for copyrighted material. Discuss your ideas in a small group.

Key Ideas
In this chapter, you will learn about
- *the* Canadian Charter of Rights and Freedoms
- *the judicial system and your rights under the law*
- *ways you can exercise your rights and responsibilities*

Rise in illegal music downloads fault of recording industry greed

Neighbour complains she can't open windows due to backyard smoker

Fear leads to code of silence in gang-related gun crimes

13-year-old faces adult sentence for violent double homicide

Overweight heart-attack patient sues Big Buns restaurant chain

TAP into Active Citizenship

In this chapter, you have the opportunity to dream about making change. Think about what actions you would take to deal with your chosen issue if you had unlimited resources and time. Who would you work with? What steps would you include in your ideal plan of action? Jot down any ideas you have as you work your way through this chapter. File your notes in your Take Action Portfolio. You will need them again at the end of this chapter to complete the next step in your culminating activity.

52   *Passport to Civics*

The Constitution

ACTIVATE YOUR THINKING

- *Why would it be important for a country to have the power to change its own constitution?*
- *Why do you think Canada thought it was important to protect the rights of citizens?*
- *Why would some countries not have these same protections for citizens?*

Canada's democratic system ensures that the government remains accountable to its citizens through elected representatives. This is called **responsible government**. The laws, conventions (informal rules), accepted practices, and principles that govern our political system developed from the British system and were laid out in the *British North America Act, 1867*. The *BNA Act* formed Canada's Constitution. In 1982, however, the Constitution was brought home to Canada and the *BNA Act, 1867* became part of the *Constitution Act, 1982*. This marked a significant turning point in Canada's history. It meant that we could now make changes to our own constitution—the supreme law of the land—without the approval of the British Parliament. More importantly, however, the *Constitution Act, 1982* included an additional piece of legislation intended to protect and uphold the rights of citizens from the policies and actions of all levels of government. This powerful, often controversial document is called the *Canadian Charter of Rights and Freedoms*.

responsible government: a government that is accountable to its citizens through elected representatives

On April 17, 1982, Prime Minister Pierre Trudeau and Queen Elizabeth II signed Canada's Constitution, which enacted the *Canadian Charter of Rights and Freedoms*. As a result, no government in Canada can pass any law without considering what the *Charter* says.

Rights and Responsibilities 53

The *Canadian Charter of Rights and Freedoms*

Canada and Canadians have had a long history of involvement in writing statements promoting the protection of basic human rights and freedoms. In 1946, New Brunswick Professor John Peters Humphrey was one of the main drafters of the Universal Declaration of Human Rights for the United Nations.

Legislation such as the *Canadian Bill of Rights* of 1960 and the *Canadian Human Rights Act* of 1977 was made into law by the federal government to protect individual rights and freedoms. Several provinces had also enacted legislation to protect civil liberties (basic human rights). But because these documents were not included in the constitution, they were not part of the supreme law of the land and could always be changed or repealed (cancelled).

> The *Charter* is such an important piece of legislation that it forms the first part of Canada's constitution. The *Charter* is divided into several sections that define the many freedoms and rights we have as Canadians.

The *Charter* also clearly recognizes the multicultural heritage of Canadians and the fact that French and English are the two official languages of Canada. Equality rights guarantee that all Canadians are treated equally before the law despite differences in race, national or ethnic origin, colour, religion, sex, age, or mental or physical disability.

The fact that the *Charter* recognizes the special status and rights of Aboriginal peoples says a great deal about the values Canadians

54   *Passport to Civics*

believe are important. Protecting the culture, customs, traditions, and languages of Aboriginal peoples is the focus of section 25 of the *Charter*. Aboriginal peoples have certain guaranteed rights under this section that other rights in the *Charter* cannot interfere with. For example, people who want the same benefits Aboriginal peoples have as a result of certain treaties cannot use section 15 of the *Charter* to argue that they have been denied the right to be treated equally. In addition, section 35 of the *Constitution Act, 1982* recognizes and protects existing Aboriginal and treaty rights dating back to 1763.

FREEDOMS AND RIGHTS UNDER THE *CHARTER*

Members of the Ontario Public Service Employees Union take part in a walkout in Sudbury to protest hospital staff shortages.

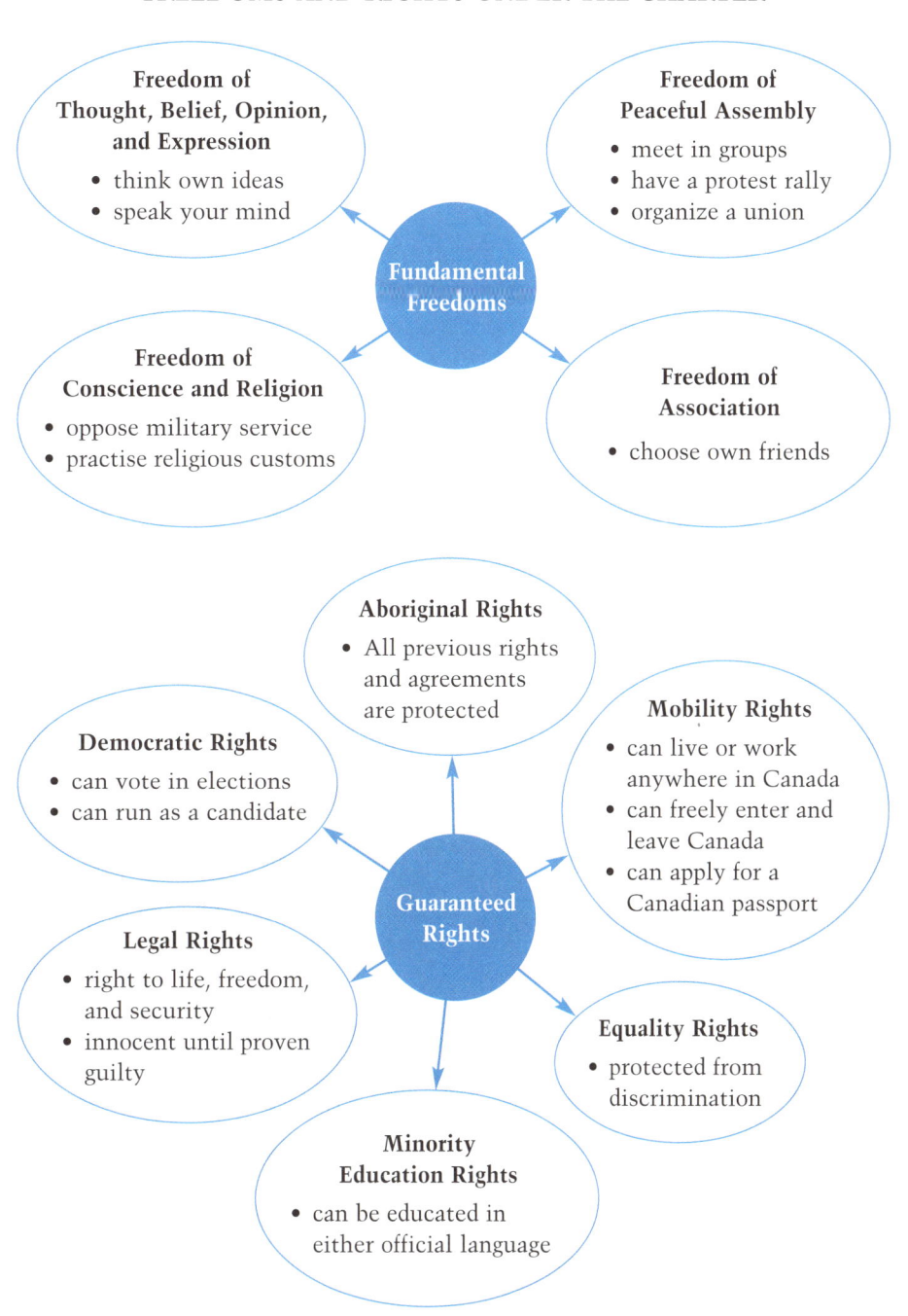

Fundamental Freedoms

Freedom of Thought, Belief, Opinion, and Expression
- think own ideas
- speak your mind

Freedom of Peaceful Assembly
- meet in groups
- have a protest rally
- organize a union

Freedom of Conscience and Religion
- oppose military service
- practise religious customs

Freedom of Association
- choose own friends

Guaranteed Rights

Aboriginal Rights
- All previous rights and agreements are protected

Democratic Rights
- can vote in elections
- can run as a candidate

Mobility Rights
- can live or work anywhere in Canada
- can freely enter and leave Canada
- can apply for a Canadian passport

Legal Rights
- right to life, freedom, and security
- innocent until proven guilty

Equality Rights
- protected from discrimination

Minority Education Rights
- can be educated in either official language

Rights and Responsibilities

Every year, Aboriginal people in many urban centres are joined by others in the community to celebrate National Aboriginal Day. This picture shows a dawn rooftop flag raising ceremony at Toronto City Hall.

WHAT CAN YOU DO?

Celebrate National Aboriginal Day

In 1982, the National Indian Brotherhood (today the Assembly of First Nations) called for the establishment of a National Aboriginal Solidarity Day. June 21 was chosen because of the cultural significance to Aboriginal peoples of the summer solstice (the longest day of the year).

National Aboriginal Day is a time to celebrate the accomplishments of Aboriginal communities in Ontario and across Canada. It is a time to treasure rich traditions and appreciate the contributions made by elders, leaders, artists and all individuals who value their Aboriginal heritage. And it is a time to look forward to changes, which will help these communities not only to survive, but to thrive.
— Honourable James K. Bartleman, former Lieutenant Governor of Ontario, June 21, 2005

The first celebrations took place in 1996. Every June 21 since then, thousands of Canadians learn about and celebrate the unique heritage and cultures of First Nations, Inuit, and Métis. Events, both formal and informal, take place across the country. These include sunrise ceremonies, parades, storytelling, and powwows (sacred celebrations, which include traditional music, dancing, and crafts).

How does the celebration of National Aboriginal Day reflect the values and beliefs of Canadians? Find out how you can participate in National Aboriginal Day in your community.

Legal Rights

Many legal experts think that the *Charter* has had the most significant impact on Canadian society in the area of criminal law. The *Charter* affects all areas of criminal law, from the investigation of a crime, fairness at trial, and decisions about the use of evidence, to the sentencing of convicted individuals. A criminal law passed by parliament can be removed if it violates one of the freedoms protected by the *Charter*, and if the government cannot justify the violation as the only reasonable way to meet an important need.

Sections 7 to 14 of the *Charter* outline the legal rights guaranteed to all people who are subject to Canadian law (citizens, visitors, and residents).

In summary, everyone has the right

- to life, liberty, and safety, and the right not to have this freedom taken away unless it is related to basic justice; (for example, the police cannot stop a driver simply because of his or her race)
- to be free from unreasonable search or arrest
- not to be stopped without reason or arrested without reason
- when arrested, to
  - be informed immediately of the reason for the arrest
  - have a lawyer without delay, and to be informed of the right to legal advice
  - have the fairness or validity of the arrest determined by **habeas corpus** and to be let go if the detention is unlawful
- when charged with an offence (crime), to
  - be informed without unreasonable delay of what the offence is
  - be given a trial within a reasonable time
  - not be forced to be a witness against yourself
  - be presumed (assumed) innocent until proven guilty according to law and a fair and public trial
  - not be denied bail without good reason
  - not be found guilty of something that happened or was done before it became illegal
  - have a trial by jury if the maximum punishment for the specific offence is five or more years
  - not be tried again for the same offence if acquitted (found not guilty), or not be tried and punished again for the same offence
- not to be treated or punished in a cruel way
- when testifying as a witness not to have anything you say used against you in other proceedings, except in the case of perjury (lying under oath)
- to an interpreter if you do not speak the language of the trial, or you are hearing impaired

As you read the following case studies, try to identify the legal rights that are not being upheld.

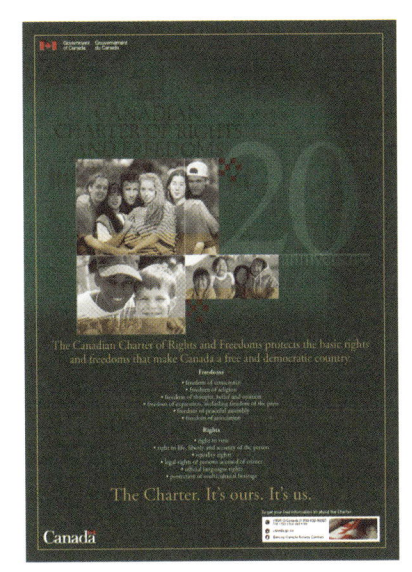

Many view the *Charter* as a symbol of the values Canadians hold dear. Would you agree? Why?

habeas corpus: an order requiring that a prisoner appear before a court to decide if his or her detention is lawful; protects against illegal imprisonment; from the Latin meaning "you have the body"

CASE STUDY 14: WRONG PLACE, WRONG TIME

Samir and Joe are walking down the street in their neighbourhood toward a park. Joe is carrying a cricket bat. A police car pulls up and the officers tell

Rights and Responsibilities 57

Samir and Joe to come along with them to the station. The officers explain that they have just received a report of a car window being smashed two blocks away, and suspect that Samir and Joe are responsible. When they arrive at the station, Samir and Joe are taken into questioning without the chance to call anyone.

CASE STUDY 15: THE SHOPLIFTER

Cheuk is stopped while leaving a department store. Her bag is searched and she is accused of shoplifting. When the police arrive, they ask her questions, then one of the officers tells her she can make a phone call. Cheuk does not understand the officer, since she speaks very limited English. When she does not choose to call anyone, the police take her away and charge her.

Notwithstanding Clause

Although minority rights and basic civil rights are guaranteed in the *Canadian Charter of Rights and Freedoms*, section 33(1) allows governments to override (ignore) certain *Charter* rights for justifiable reasons. Called the *notwithstanding clause*, this part of the *Charter* has been controversial since its inclusion.

A number of provinces wanted it included before they would agree to the passing of the *Charter* in the Constitution. Under the *BNA Act* of 1867, the provinces had the power to legislate over civil rights. If the *Charter* did not have a notwithstanding clause, the provinces would lose this jurisdiction (control), which they were not willing to do. Any *Charter* right that is overridden with the notwithstanding clause has a time limit of five years, subject to renewal. Saskatchewan, for example, used the notwithstanding clause to end a legal strike. Alberta used it to protect an exclusively heterosexual definition of marriage. However, Alberta could not enforce the decision because marriage falls under federal rather than provincial jurisdiction. Québec used it to restrict the freedom of non-English speaking students to choose if they wished to receive their education, an area of provincial authority, in English.

APPLY YOUR LEARNING

1. Choose one of the fundamental freedoms. Explain in a paragraph why you think it is important to protect it. Give examples to support your ideas.
2. a) Rewrite Case Study 14 or 15 so that all relevant legal rights are upheld.
   b) Role-play the new case study with a partner.
3. Why should it be important to Canadians that the *Charter* recognizes and accepts previous agreements with Aboriginal peoples? Share your thoughts with a partner.

4. Examine the following photos. What rights and freedoms are being demonstrated in each photo?

The Judicial System

ACTIVATE YOUR THINKING

*The words **judge** and **justice** are related to the word **judicial**. With that in mind, list at least five words or phrases that would describe what you expect from the Canadian judicial system. Add your ideas to a class list.*

judge: the person who is in charge of a trial in a court, and who decides how a person who is found guilty should be punished

justice: the system for putting the law into action; the justice system

judicial: anything relating to a court or system of law

Although the judiciary is one of the three branches of government in Canada, under the Constitution it is separate and independent from the executive and legislative branches. This is an important feature of a free and democratic society. The significant power of the judiciary to settle disputes, interpret laws, and uphold our Constitution requires that it remain a neutral body, free from government interference.

The Rule of Law

rule of law: everyone, no matter who they are, is subject to the same laws

The principle or belief that is the cornerstone of the judicial system of Canada is the **rule of law**. This means that all written laws and unwritten but accepted rules of practice (called *conventions*) apply equally to everyone, from the general public to members of law enforcement agencies, from the military to governments and government officials. The rule of law ensures the safety and protection of our rights and freedoms.

The document that introduced the principle of the rule of law was the *Magna Carta* (Great Charter), which was signed in England in 1215. The *Magna Carta* was intended to hold the king answerable to the law

Rights and Responsibilities 59

of the land. Because Canada's parliamentary system and constitution are rooted in British law, the principle continues to this day. In Canada, the rule of law means that

- all people, even the most important or powerful, must obey the same laws
- the government itself must obey the laws that it makes and be answerable to the people. If the laws it makes are unacceptable, a government can be defeated through a democratic election.
- all members of the judicial system, such as police, lawyers, and judges, must not only uphold the laws of the land, but also obey them. Discipline, job loss, or criminal charges could result from decisions or actions not in keeping with the rule of law.

Not surprisingly, authoritarian nations do not follow the rule of law. Society in these countries is divided into law makers and those who must obey the law.

CITIZEN IN ACTION

Nelson Mandela

apartheid: an official policy that denies certain groups political, legal, and economic equality, keeping people separated based on their racial or cultural differences

Nelson Mandela was born in South Africa in 1918. Trained as a lawyer, he has worked tirelessly throughout his entire life against his country's policies of racial division and oppression. **Apartheid** was the official policy of the Republic of South Africa that kept whites and non-whites segregated (separated). Non-whites were discriminated against politically, legally, economically, and socially. They were not allowed to vote, and had limited access to education, justice, and employment opportunities.

Mandela opposed apartheid in non-violent ways, joining the Youth League of the African National Congress. Later he was actively involved in campaigns of passive resistance (non-violent acts) against the laws that kept Blacks deprived of their rights. Despite spending almost three decades in prison for his efforts, Mandela remained firm in his commitment to democracy, equality, and education.

In 1993, Nelson Mandela was awarded the Nobel Peace Prize.

> I have cherished the ideal of a democratic and free society in which all persons live together in harmony and with equal opportunities. It is an ideal which I hope to live for and to achieve. But if needs be, it is an ideal for which I am prepared to die.
>
> — Nelson Mandela, at his 1964 trial

With the elimination of apartheid, Mandela became president of a new South Africa and helped his country face its past.

Plan an appropriate celebration of the actions of Nelson Mandela.

Mr. Justice Kofi N. Barnes, Ontario Court of Justice (Oshawa) is a native of Ghana, West Africa. He was one of the founders of Toronto's Drug Treatment Court. Recently, there has been some discussion about whether judges should be elected rather than appointed. Give two reasons why people might want judges to be elected.

Jury: a group of people chosen from the community who hear the facts of a case and decide on the guilt or innocence of the accused

appellate court: a higher court that has the power to review and overturn the decision made by a lower court

Judges, Juries, and the Court System

Judges are legal experts, who ensure that law-making and law enforcement are properly carried out. They settle disputes according to law, including disputes about how the powers of the other two branches of government—the legislative and executive—are exercised. It is essential that judges make decisions based on fact and law alone, which is why they must be independent of political influence.

Judges in Canada are appointed by either the federal or provincial government. Appointments are made from a panel of candidates within the legal field. Historically, these appointments tend to be free of political bias.

To safeguard judicial independence, judges
- remain on the bench (preside over a court) until they retire
- are well paid to protect against bribery
- are assigned cases by the Chief Justice

Judges also instruct juries on the law. A **jury** is a group of people chosen from the community who hear the facts of a case and decide on the guilt or innocence of the accused. Juries usually consist of 12 adults, both males and females. They are chosen from a random pool of citizens, who have no links to the justice system. Police officers, employees in the correctional system, and people who have been formerly convicted of a crime, among others, are not eligible to serve on a jury.

Jury duty can range in length from a week to several months, depending on the case. Jury members must not have any knowledge of the accused to ensure that the verdict (conclusion) they reach is not biased (influenced). Under Section 11(f) of the *Canadian Charter of Rights and Freedoms*, individuals accused of the most serious criminal offences can choose to be tried by a jury or by a judge alone. However, it is up to the judge to determine the sentence (punishment) a convicted individual must receive.

Judges are in charge of many different types of courts and not all courts use the jury system. Canada's court system is complex, because the federal, provincial, and territorial governments have the power to make laws. Each level of government shares the responsibility for staffing and maintaining the various courts. However, only the Supreme Court of Canada and federally created courts, such as the Tax Court of Canada, are the exclusive responsibility of the federal government.

If either side in a court case feels that an error has been made, it can ask a provincial or territorial **appellate court** to hear the case. If the ruling is still in question, either side can appeal the case to the Supreme Court of Canada—the highest and final court of appeal.

The Supreme Court of Canada has nine Supreme Court judges to guard against a split decision. Not every case that reaches the Supreme Court of Canada is heard by all nine judges; however, every case is

It is your civic duty to respond when you are summoned to a jury pool, and if you are chosen, to serve on a jury. Jury duty is another important method of citizen participation in a democracy. Many people think serving on juries is inconvenient, yet it is essential to ensuring that a fair process occurs and that the rights of an accused are protected.

Madame Justice Beverley McLachlin became the 17th Chief Justice of the Supreme Court of Canada in January 2000, and the first woman in Canadian history to head the highest court in the land.

heard by an odd number of judges to ensure that a decision is reached. The *Supreme Court Act* requires that three of the nine judges be appointed from Québec. Traditionally, the federal government appoints three judges from Ontario, two from the West, and one from Atlantic Canada. Supreme Court judges have experience in different courts, usually at the provincial level, and have demonstrated superior skill in interpreting and applying the laws of Canada wisely and fairly.

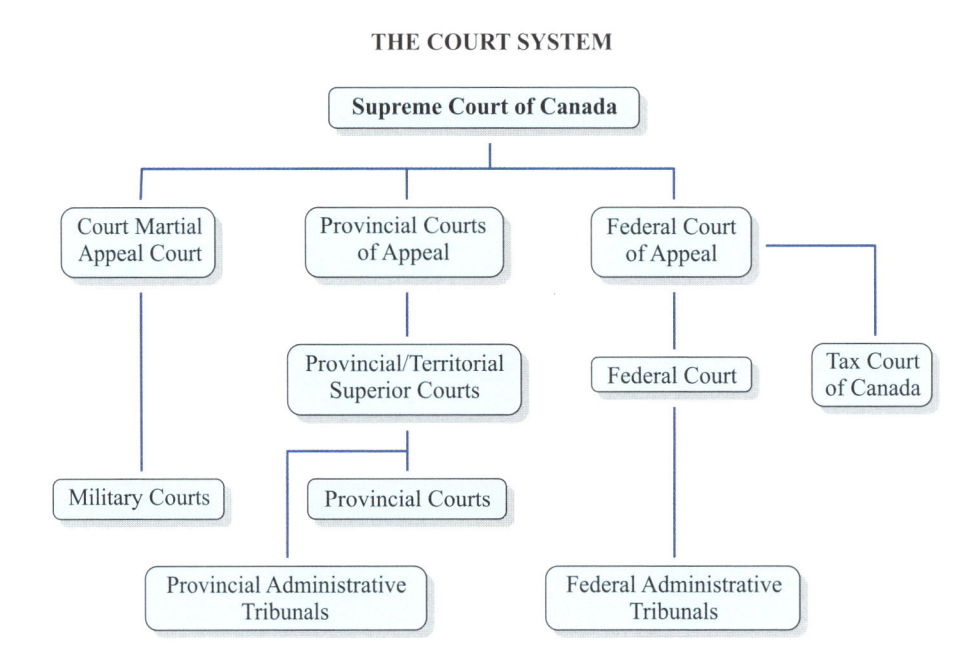

THE COURT SYSTEM

- Supreme Court of Canada
  - Court Martial Appeal Court
    - Military Courts
  - Provincial Courts of Appeal
    - Provincial/Territorial Superior Courts
      - Provincial Courts
        - Provincial Administrative Tribunals
  - Federal Court of Appeal
    - Federal Court
      - Federal Administrative Tribunals
    - Tax Court of Canada

Criminal courts hear disputes between individuals and the state, and determine the guilt or innocence of those accused of criminal

62   *Passport to Civics*

acts. Civil courts hear disputes between individuals, and then decide which of the two parties is in the right. In civil cases there is no guilt or innocence. When resolving disputes, judges interpret the law and make decisions that convey what is acceptable behaviour and what the law really intends.

Most disputes do not even end up in the courts, as it is often easier, faster, and less costly to seek other dispute-resolution methods. In fact, people are encouraged to seek these less formal means of settling their differences. In such cases, past court rulings will often affect the decisions people make. These methods include **mediation**, where an independent third party is brought in to help work out an agreement, and **arbitration**, where both sides agree to refer the dispute to a third party for judgment.

30

mediation: a process of resolving disputes in which an independent third party helps two or more parties work toward a solution that is acceptable to all parties

arbitration: a process of resolving disputes in which the parties involved refer their problem to a knowledgeable, independent third party (an arbitrator) and agree in advance to accept the arbitrator's decision

APPLY YOUR LEARNING

1. a) Create a spider diagram in your notebook following the model below. For each category, list two or three points that would help someone understand our judicial system better.
   b) Compare your completed organizer with that of a partner. Add points from his or her diagram that are not already listed on yours.

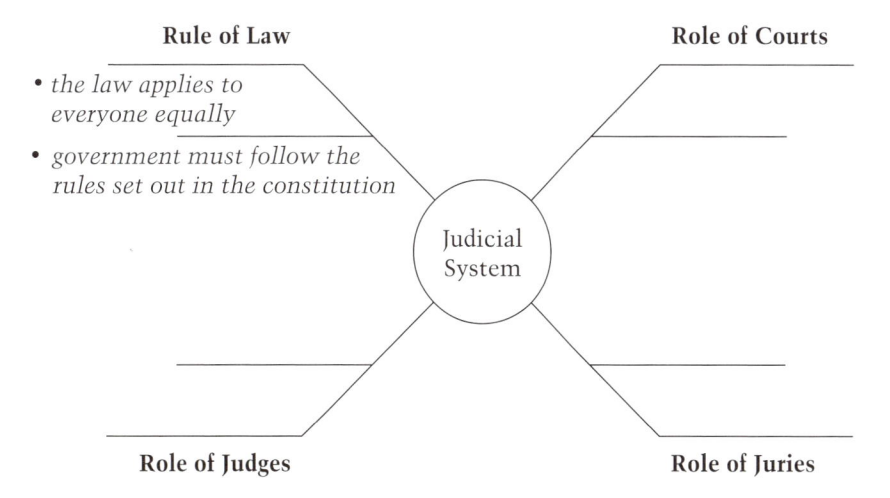

Rule of Law
- *the law applies to everyone equally*
- *government must follow the rules set out in the constitution*

Role of Courts

Judicial System

Role of Judges

Role of Juries

Newspaper articles: all newspaper articles answer the 5Ws+H, usually in the first couple of paragraphs.
   Scanning is a way of quickly reading down a page, list, paragraph, or article to find a specific word, detail, or fact. We scan when we read for some information we need without having to read the whole text.
   Skimming is a way of quickly reading across a text to get the main idea and some details. We skim to get an overall sense of the text, (for example, to find out if it has information that we can use, or if we are interested in the topic).

2. Find a newspaper article related to a court case and attach it to a page in your notebook.
   a) Highlight any references to the court, the judge, the jury, and the *Charter*.
   b) Answer the questions *who*, *what*, *when*, *where*, *how*, and if possible, *why*.
   c) Retitle the article to reflect what you consider to be the main idea or point of the article.
3. a) List three reasons why you would want a jury deciding your innocence or guilt.
   b) Under what circumstances do you think it would be better to have a judge alone hear your case?

Rights and Responsibilities

Rights Abused, Restricted, and Upheld

ACTIVATE YOUR THINKING

Brainstorm with the class any situations you can think of in which the rights of the group should have priority over the rights of an individual. In what situations should individual rights have priority over collective rights? Create a T-chart to record the results of the discussion.

Collective Rights should override individual rights when...	Individual Rights should override collective rights when...

Canada continues to be a world leader in upholding the rights of its citizens. There are occasions, however, when the rights of Canadians are violated, especially when there are conflicts between individual and collective rights. Individual rights are your own distinct and separate rights, whereas collective rights refer to the rights enjoyed by a group.

The government has also been guilty of rights violations, but has shown leadership in admitting past errors and providing compensation to victims. This can be seen in the January 2007 decision to apologize and pay $10.5 million in compensation to Maher Arar. This Canadian of Syrian background was unjustly deported to Syria, partly based on Canadian accusations of his links to terrorist movements. In Syria he was imprisoned and tortured.

The section of the *Canadian Charter of Rights and Freedoms* that deals with equality rights reads as follows:

> 15. (1) Every individual is equal before and under the law and has the right to the equal protection and equal benefit of the law without discrimination [unfair treatment] and, in particular, without discrimination based on race, national or ethnic origin, colour, religion, sex, age or mental or physical disability.
> (2) Subsection (1) does not preclude [prevent or disqualify] any law, program or activity that has as its object the amelioration [making better or improving] of conditions of disadvantaged individuals or groups including those that are disadvantaged because of race, national or ethnic origin, colour, religion, sex, age or mental or physical disability.

Reread the passage on equality rights and list all the categories that are protected. Beside each one, identify it as an individual right or as a collective right. Are there any individuals or groups of people that the *Charter* does not protect?

There have been times in Canadian history when certain groups of people did not have equal rights. This happened because the beliefs and values that people held in the past were different from those

Prime Minister Stephen Harper issued a formal apology to Maher Arar (pictured with his wife, Monia Mazigh) for the role Canada played in Arar's 2002 deportation and subsequent torture in a Syrian prison.

Canadians believe and value today. Fortunately, our judicial system has the power to change or repeal laws that no longer represent current principles and viewpoints.

As you read through the cases that follow, try to identify which part of the *Charter* would ensure such rights abuses would not happen today.

CASE STUDY 16: CHINESE HEAD TAX

In 1902, a Royal Commission on Chinese and Japanese Immigration labelled Asians "unfit for full citizenship." Chinese immigrants were forced to pay a head tax (a per-person fee) to enter Canada, which restricted immigration and kept those already here from bringing loved ones to Canada.

CASE STUDY 17: THE "PERSONS" CASE

In 1928, the Supreme Court of Canada ruled that women were not "persons" under the law and could not be named to the Senate. The British Privy Council, the British version of the Supreme Court, was able to overturn this ruling because at that time our Constitution was still an Act of the British government. This meant their supreme court had authority over ours.

CASE STUDY 18: INTERNMENT OF JAPANESE-CANADIANS

During World War II, the government legislated that Japanese-Canadians be forced from their homes and sent to isolated camps (called *internment camps*). They were held in these camps for the remainder of the war. The government also seized their possessions and sold them for much less than they were worth.

Japanese-Canadians were forcibly relocated to internment camps in the interior of British Columbia during World War II. If you were assigned to take a photo such as this, what would you focus on to show you were sympathetic to the plight of Japanese-Canadians?

Rights and Responsibilities

Aboriginal children between the ages of 5 and 16 were taken from their families and sent to residential boarding schools in various parts of Canada. Would school officials be pleased with this photo? Would Aboriginal peoples? Explain your thinking to a partner.

These people, led by a young boy, did not survive the war in Nazi-occupied Europe. We see them here in Warsaw, Poland, in April 1943, on their way to an assembly point at a railway station. There they will be deported to a death camp, where the Nazis will kill them. What expressions do you see on the faces of the children? The adults? The soldiers?

CASE STUDY 19: TREATMENT OF PEOPLE WITH DISABILITIES

Until the early 1970s, Alberta and British Columbia had laws that allowed the sterilization (surgical removal of reproductive organs) of those deemed "mentally defective" without individual or family consent. The criteria for determining "mentally defective" were unreliable and invalid.

CASE STUDY 20: TREATMENT OF ABORIGINAL PEOPLES

For almost 100 years, it was customary for the children of Aboriginal peoples to be separated from their families and communities and taken to special schools to live. Many of the children who were sent to residential schools suffered various forms of abuse at the hands of those who ran the schools. First Nations people were also denied the right to vote until 1960.

With the enactment of the *Charter of Rights and Freedoms* in our constitution, rights abuses are less common. What can happen, however, is the restriction of individual rights and freedoms in favour of collective rights. A significant case in which *Charter* rights were restricted involved a high school history teacher from Alberta. As you read the following case study, think about which right is more important: freedom of expression or freedom from discrimination.

CASE STUDY 21: THE KEEGSTRA CASE

Eckville, Alberta, high school teacher (and one-time mayor), James Keegstra, taught students in his history class that the Holocaust—the systematic murder of millions of Jewish people by the Nazis during World War II—never occurred. He also made many untrue statements about Jewish people.

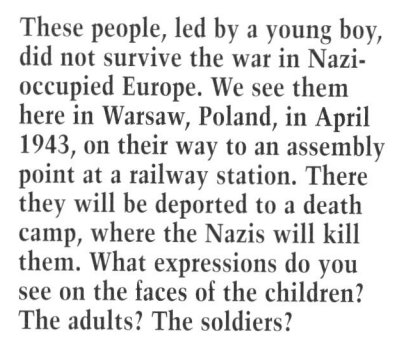

Keegstra was charged in 1984 under section 319(2) of the Criminal Code (the book that defines everything that is a crime in Canada) with promoting hatred against an identifiable group and making anti-Semitic statements. He was found guilty and ordered to pay a fine of $5000. On appeal he cited the *Charter* right to freedom of expression, claiming it permitted him to say what he wanted. The case went all the way to the Supreme Court of Canada. In

66   *Passport to Civics*

Simon Wiesenthal was one of millions of Jewish people persecuted by the Nazis during World War II and one of the few to survive the death camps. He dedicated his life after the war to rooting out Nazi war criminals who went into hiding all around the world. By documenting the crimes of the Holocaust and working tirelessly to bring the perpetrators to justice, Wiesenthal raised awareness of the need to confront hate, defend human rights, and promote tolerance.

Reading graphs: similar to charts, graphs help readers and audiences understand data at a glance, identify trends, and translate data into meaningful information. The title tells you what the graph is about. The labels help you to interpret the information. *Bar graphs* compare values. *Line graphs* compare data over time. *Pie graphs* show parts of a whole as percentages. Simple pie graphs (those that do not have too many categories) are a clear way of comparing values.

The survey also revealed that over half of the hate crimes motivated by race or ethnicity involved direct attacks on a person, whereas most religion-based hate crimes were acts of vandalism. However, individuals targeted because of sexual orientation were more likely than any other group to suffer violent crimes. What questions do you have about the information in the graph? Where could you find answers to these questions?

1996, the Supreme Court said that the guarantee of freedom of expression couldn't be more important than the right of Canadians not to be subjected to discrimination. In this case, the collective rights of Jewish people to freedom from discrimination were considered greater than the individual right of James Keegstra to freedom of expression. The Alberta Court of Appeal overturned Keegstra's original sentence, which was not addressed by the Supreme Court. The $5000 fine was replaced with a one-year suspended sentence (prison time that does not have to be served provided certain conditions are met), a year of probation, and 200 hours of community-service work.

WHAT CAN YOU DO?

Stand Up to Hate

Like an unchecked cancer, hate corrodes the personality and eats away its vital unity. Hate destroys a man's sense of values and his objectivity. It causes him to describe the beautiful as ugly and the ugly as beautiful, and to confuse the true with the false and the false with the true.
— Martin Luther King, Jr., US civil rights leader (1929–1968)

In Canada, the Criminal Code says a hate crime is an action intended to intimidate (bully or threaten), harm, or terrify a person or an entire group of people based on race, religion, gender, ethnicity, ability, or sexual orientation. Hate crimes involve intimidation, harassment, physical force, or threat of physical force against a person, family, or property.

During a 2001–2002 pilot survey of 12 major police forces across Canada, 928 hate crimes were reported. The bar graph below identifies the percentage of those crimes that were targeted toward people based on their race, religion, or sexual orientation.

SURVEY OF HATE CRIME IN CANADA 2001–2002

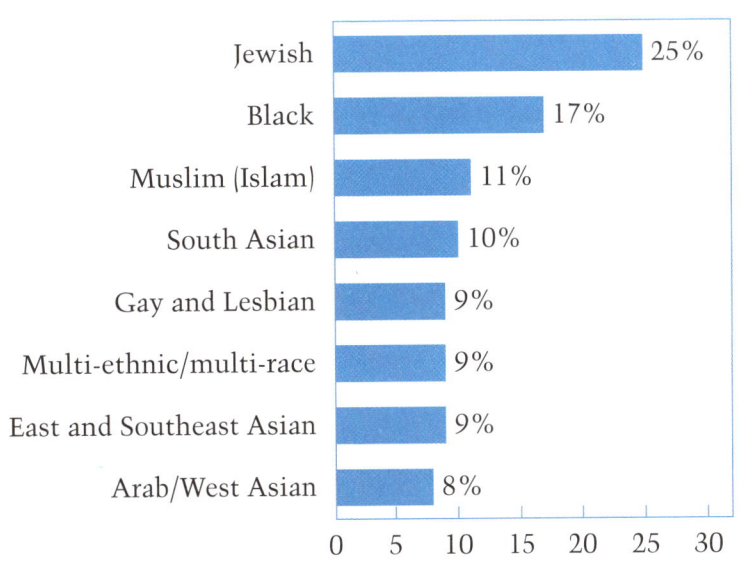

Group	Percentage
Jewish	25%
Black	17%
Muslim (Islam)	11%
South Asian	10%
Gay and Lesbian	9%
Multi-ethnic/multi-race	9%
East and Southeast Asian	9%
Arab/West Asian	8%

Source: *Statistics Canada*

Rights and Responsibilities

Azmi Jubran, a British Columbia high school student, was bullied and harassed by his peers over several years. He was called names, punched, pushed, spat on, and had objects thrown at him. In June 1996, Jubran filed a complaint with the British Columbia Human Rights Commission because the school did not fully deal with the problem. Although the school punished the students involved each time an incident occurred, the bullying and harassment continued. In 2005, the British Columbia Court of Appeal decided that schools and school boards must provide a safe learning environment, free from harassment. They must take actions to prevent bullying, not simply wait for it to occur before taking action. When Azmi Jubran filed his complaint, he stood up not only for his own rights, but also for the rights of all students.

We all have a part to play in standing up to and preventing hate in our community. Here are some ways you can take action:
- Speak out against jokes and slurs that target certain people or groups.
- Find ways to celebrate diversity.
- Do not exclude people because they may seem different from you. Welcome newcomers to your school or community.
- Avoid stereotypical comments, and challenge others who make them.
- Learn more about other cultures and their traditions.
- Research the struggle for rights and freedoms around the world.
- Report to school officials or the police any actions that promote hatred.
- Join clubs or community organizations that are working to fight hate and bias.

According to the Canadian Civil Liberties Association, "The freedom of no one is safe unless the freedom of everyone is safe." Create a public service announcement (PSA) that educates others about what this statement means.

Privacy Rights and You

Have you ever thought about how much of your life is not private? Some schools have cameras in the halls. Many malls and most government buildings do as well. What about the information you enter in contests to win a prize? Or the mail you receive that includes your name and address? How does your family protect that information?

The Internet is probably the least private place you can go. Cookies and other devices track where you go and how long you spend there. Using debit and credit cards also puts your privacy and personal information at risk.

So, how protected do you think your privacy is? Take the quiz that follows to find out. For each statement, answer True or False.

Study this photo. Create a three-column chart in your notebook. In the first column, state what you see. In the second, describe what it makes you think of. In the third, explain what you wonder about now that you have seen this image.

PRIVACY QUIZ

1. My e-mail is private and cannot be read by others. When I delete it, it is gone forever.
2. Businesses cannot ask for my Health card as identification.
3. The government can use personal information it has about me to freeze my bank accounts.
4. My locker is private property and cannot be opened by anyone but my locker partner or me.
5. My Internet activities can be tracked.
6. Papers and envelopes with my name and address on them can be safely thrown into the recycling bin, since there isn't much anyone can do with just that information anyway.

Discuss your responses with a partner before checking the correct answers at the bottom of this page. Which answers, if any, surprised you? Which answer did you find most troubling?

Access to Information

For a democracy to work, the government must be as open to the public as possible. This openness goes beyond citizens being welcome as visitors in government buildings. It means the government will tell you what you want to know. Contrast this with an authoritarian system of government that gives you only the information it wants you to have.

However, an equally important feature of a democratic government is protecting information that is not intended to be public. The newspaper, your neighbour, or the letter carrier have no right to your health information, school records, or bank account numbers. In Ontario, finding the balance between openness and privacy is the responsibility of the Information and Privacy Commissioner (IPC).

CITIZEN IN ACTION

Ann Cavoukian

After receiving her M.A. and Ph.D. in Psychology from the University of Toronto, where she specialized in criminology and law, Dr. Ann Cavoukian went on to become Ontario's Information and Privacy Commissioner (IPC). She has held the post since 1998. An outspoken defender of privacy rights, Ann Cavoukian is responsible for both the provincial and municipal Freedom of Information and Privacy laws, as well as the *Personal Health Information Protection Act*. Although the explosion in information technology in the early 1990s had a major impact on the whole issue of privacy and how we safeguard

Ann Cavoukian, Information and Privacy Commissioner, Ontario

1. False 2. True 3. True 4. False 5. True 6. False

Rights and Responsibilities

What is the message behind this image? How does it make you feel?

it, Ann Cavoukian is a strong believer in using technology to help protect privacy. Many businesses in North America and Europe now seek her advice and guidance on privacy and data protection issues.

Ann Cavoukian believes public access to government records "is one of the most important rights of a democratic society." Her role as IPC requires her to

- answer appeals when the government refuses to provide information
- investigate privacy complaints about information held by government organizations
- ensure that government organizations follow the access and privacy rules
- educate the public about Ontario's access and privacy laws
- carry out research on access and privacy issues, and provide advice on proposed government legislation and programs

Ann Cavoukian speaks around the world on the importance of privacy, and has co-authored two books on the topic: *Who Knows: Safeguarding Your Privacy in a Networked World* and *The Privacy Payoff: How Successful Businesses Build Customer Trust.*

Select one of the tasks for which the IPC is responsible, and explain in a paragraph how or where it could affect your life personally. Look back at the quiz on page 69 for hints.

When personal information is not handled correctly or government information is not made available, the IPC will investigate and make recommendations to prevent similar events from happening in the future.

Here are two recent examples that involved the IPC:

"Medical records found scattered across Toronto streets:
Commissioner Cavoukian issues first Order under new law"

NEWS RELEASE: July 25, 2005
"Commissioner orders City of Toronto to release lawsuit information."

Under the *Freedom of Information and Protection of Privacy Act* or the *Municipal Freedom of Information and Protection of Privacy Act*, you can access any information held by government organizations unless it is under exemption. For example, cabinet minutes (notes taken during cabinet meetings), or information that, if shared, would violate another person's rights, are exempt. It is important in a democracy that exemptions are specific and clearly stated, and that the privacy of individuals is protected.

Information that is available to the public might be on paper, microfilm, or computer disk, and could include photographs and even maps.

The easiest way to access information from the government is to ask for it in writing, by phone, or by going to the government organization, office, or department involved. If that doesn't work, make a Freedom of Information request, identifying which of the two Acts you are using (either provincial or municipal). Send the request to the Freedom of Information and Privacy Commissioner. There is a small application fee, payable to the Minister of Finance.

APPLY YOUR LEARNING

---

1. a) Research one of the rights abuse cases (Case Studies 16 to 20) to find answers to the following questions:
    - Why was the law changed?
    - What does the law say today about this issue?
    - What apology or compensation, if any, was provided to those affected?

   b) Prepare a report to share with the class. Consider creating a visual display, which includes pictures, relevant quotations, and other key information.

2. Complete the following organizer in your notebook to record your thoughts about the Keegstra case (Case Study 21). Do you think James Keegstra received a fair punishment for his actions? Do you think freedom from discrimination is more important than freedom of expression?

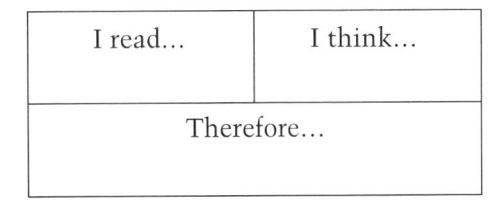

I read...	I think...
Therefore...	

3. a) Find a recent case in which the Information and Privacy Commissioner has been involved. Prepare a brace map like the one below to organize key information about the case.

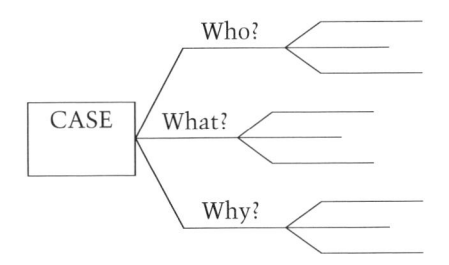

   CASE — Who? / What? / Why?

Rights and Responsibilities 71

b) Write a summary of the case using information in your organizer. A summary has
- an opening paragraph that introduces the topic with some key ideas
- two or three paragraphs that contain supporting details on the topic, with added details to expand it
- a concluding (final) paragraph that brings all the points together

Arrange the ideas in your summary in order of importance (from most to least), or in chronological order (the order in which the events occurred) if that is relevant. Include only important information, not trivial or unrelated details.

Canada's Youth Justice System

ACTIVATE YOUR THINKING

Create a K-W-L chart in your notebook. Record what you know and what you want to know about the youth criminal justice system in Canada. Then, predict what you think you will learn as you read through this section.

What I Know	What I Want to Know	What I Have Learned

KWL charts: KWL charts help to focus your reading. Work with other students or individually to complete a chart with these three headings:
- What do I/we **know** about this topic?
- What do I/we **want** to know?
- What did I/we **learn**?

Under Canadian law, people under the age of 18 who have committed crimes are treated differently from adults (those over 18).

The *Youth Criminal Justice Act* (YCJA), which is the most recent law for youth aged 12 to 17, became law in 2003, replacing the *Young Offenders Act* (YOA). The main purpose of the YCJA is to
- prevent youth crime by addressing the circumstances that lead to offending behaviours
- separate youth justice from the adult system
- ensure that the rights and privacy of youth are protected
- intervene quickly when a crime is committed to ensure that there is a clear connection between the offence and the consequence
- hold youths accountable for their actions by providing relevant and meaningful sentences (consequences) that reflect not only the seriousness of the crime, but also the age and maturity of the accused
- reform and bring youths back into society by providing the necessary treatment and support needed to help them become productive members of the community

This illustration was created by self-taught Mohawk artist Garrison Garrow. According to Garrow, "Problems amongst the youth are a reflection of problems within the community." How does this illustration reflect the principles behind restorative justice?

- encourage the involvement and co-operation of victims, families, volunteer organizations, teachers, and psychologists, in addition to the justice system

Restorative justice is one approach to dealing with youth crime that has its origins in the traditions of Aboriginal peoples. Governments, community organizations, interest groups, and even courts are now embracing this approach as they look for more constructive ways to deal with youth offenders. The main purpose of the formal justice system is to decide innocence or guilt. Those who have been affected have no voice in the process. In restorative justice, the focus is on healing relationships and repairing the damage crime causes to individuals and communities. It includes everyone affected by the crime. The offender must participate voluntarily and take responsibility for his or her actions. The best results occur when the victim and the offender, their families, and the community work together to resolve the issues that led to the offender's behaviour.

The police or the Crown refer cases to this system, but a representative of the Community Justice Forum (CJF) must determine if the case is suited to this approach.

CITIZEN IN ACTION

Cindy Blackstock

Cindy Blackstock is the Executive Director of the First Nations Child and Family Caring Society of Canada, and a member of Gitksan First Nation. She has advocated for "courageous conversations," which she defines as discussions about justice and what we want to happen differently in the future. She is continually challenging Canadians to think about the quality of life for First Nations children, and to make it a reality for the next generation.

Using Cindy Blackstock's idea of a "courageous conversation," select an issue that is important to you and that you think needs attention in your community. Prepare to defend your choice in a conversation with a peer.

Cindy Blackstock, Executive Director of the First Nations Child and Family Caring Society of Canada

Under the YCJA, youths are processed differently from adults accused of similar offences.

Stage	Youth Justice System	Adult Justice System
Arrest	Parents/guardians must be informed when youths are arrested and detained.	Suspect is arrested, advised of his or her rights, and given the chance to make one phone call.

Rights and Responsibilities

Stage	Youth Justice System	Adult Justice System
Laying of charges	Pre-screening by the police and consent from the Attorney General may need to be obtained before a young person is charged with an offence.	May be taken to the police station where formal charges are laid. May be given a "promise to appear" notice (come back later) or placed in custody. If placed in custody, must have a show cause hearing (bail) within 24 hours.
Trial	Cases are heard by a judge alone in special youth courts. Previously, under a serious charge, youth would be transferred to an adult court, which could delay the trial. Now, youth courts can give an adult sentence, which is longer than youth sentences.	Cases are heard by judges or juries in adult courts.
Sentencing on conviction	Sentences for crimes tend to be shorter. For example, in the case of first-degree murder (murder that is planned and deliberate), the maximum sentence is 10 years, with a maximum of 6 years in detention (in custody) and 4 years under the supervision of a probation officer.	Sentences for more serious offences tend to be much longer and are based on the Criminal Code. For example, the minimum sentence for first-degree murder in the Criminal Code is 25 years.
Detention	Jail is intended to be a last resort. Open custody (such as a group home), probation, or a combination of the two are the more common forms of detention.	Jail (if the Criminal Code requires it), or conditional sentences (house arrest) but not probation (community supervision)
Goal	Rehabilitation and reintegration into society	Rehabilitation and reintegration into society

The quotations that follow outline a variety of perspectives on the issue of youth violence. Summarize the key ideas in a T-chart like the one below. Put an asterisk (*) beside the opinions you agree with.

Ideas That Support Stiff Sentences	Ideas That Support Solving Problems

"All too often children who end up in the criminal justice system come from homes where poverty is their biggest hurdle to realizing and achieving a further education.... [A]ll youth have potential and if given an opportunity to succeed academically, these youth can become educated, responsible and contributing members of society. All they need is a second chance."
— Rick Gosling, founder, Second Chance

Toronto Mayor David Miller noted that both enforcement and prevention are necessary ingredients in solving the problem of violent gangs. *"All neighbourhoods should prosper; all kids should have a sense of meaning. The city is predominately safe, but we can't let it be taken away by guns and gangs."*

"Some of these kids are too far gone for help, but so many are just being initiated into this lifestyle and we need to rescue them. We have to."
— Monica Willie, Ontario community worker and grandmother

"It is clear that the way to heal society of its violence...and lack of love is to replace the pyramid of domination with the circle of equality and respect."
— Manintonquat, Elder of the Assonet Band of the Wampanoag Nation

Don't do the crime, if you can't do the time.
— Saying popularized by television and music

"It's terrible what's happening. When a teenager is arrested and he goes to court and they almost just slap him on the wrist and let him go and he just does it over again? You hear that every night on the news, and I think they should serve their time."
— Margaret Brown, 85-year-old Ontario resident

"All the evidence on mandatory minimum sentences—and there are tons of studies—suggests that they do not have an impact on crime. Increasing the severity of sentences does not have a deterrent effect."
— Rosemary Barton, Professor, University of Toronto's Centre of Criminology

"If we treat and view these kids as thugs then they will act like thugs (and) by giving them harsher penalties, they are going to be even greater thugs in our and their own eyes."
— Bryce Barfoot, a 22-year-old Ontario business student

Find someone in your class who has an opposing viewpoint from you on the issue of youth violence. Using the ideas you both asterisked in your charts, role-play your ideas.

CITIZENS IN ACTION

The Toronto Argonauts

In response to increased gun violence in the Greater Toronto Area in 2005, the Toronto Argonauts football team rallied a small group of concerned citizens together to address the problem. The goal of their "Stop the Violence—We Are Toronto" campaign is to
- reduce gun violence
- build the self-confidence and self-esteem of youth through mentoring
- teach young people about the risks of involvement with guns and gangs
- support youth-led violence prevention and intervention programs

Linebacker Chuck Winters experienced gang violence first hand while growing up in Detroit, Michigan. As an adolescent, Chuck Winters sought group acceptance through organized team sports rather than through gangs. But he knows what it's like to walk the streets in fear; his younger brother was murdered in a drive-by shooting in 1998.

Like many of his teammates who grew up in communities ravaged by guns, gangs, and drugs, Chuck Winters is determined to help the youth of Toronto break the cycle of violence.

"When I came to play for the Argos, I was so impressed with the city and all it has to offer. I don't want to see Toronto lose all that good and I want to help ensure that doesn't happen."
— Chuck Winters, Linebacker, Toronto Argonauts

Consider the actions of the Toronto Argonaut organization from the perspective of civic duty and evaluate its members' efforts. Research to find out what new actions they are currently taking.

Chuck Winters, Linebacker, Toronto Argonauts

APPLY YOUR LEARNING
---

1. Prepare a Venn diagram (see page 11) to compare how a youth and an adult are treated when charged with an offence.
2. Write a letter to your MP, explaining whether you agree with special treatment for youth or not, and why you have that opinion.

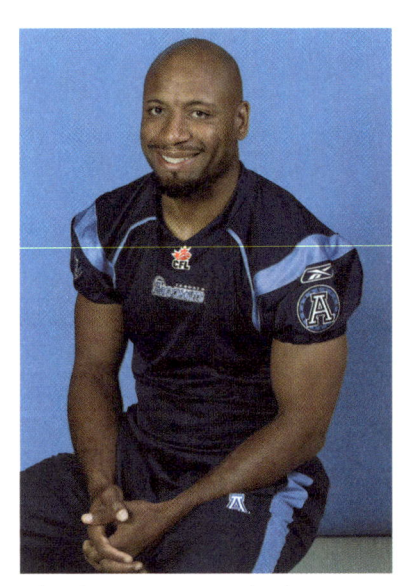

3. For each of the following scenarios, identify who should be involved in determining the punishment and what you think the punishment should be.
   a) A teenage hockey player dies as a result of injuries sustained in an on-ice fight with an opposing player.
   b) A 13-year-old conspires with a friend to poison her grandmother, who is her legal guardian, to gain the inheritance money.
   c) A 15-year-old hacks into the website of a major online retailer, shutting it down for three days.
4. a) Go back to the K-W-L chart you created at the beginning of this section (see page 72). Were your predictions about what you would learn correct? Add any new information you learned to the third column.
   b) Add a fourth column to your chart. Head this column, How Can I Find Out More? Brainstorm with a partner or small group where you might go for more information about the youth criminal justice system in Canada. List the ideas in the fourth column.

The Responsibilities of Citizenship

ACTIVATE YOUR THINKING

What responsibilities do you think someone should fulfill as a citizen of Canada? What about as a citizen of the world? List your ideas in your notebook.

You no doubt have gained certain rights and freedoms in your life both at home and at school. Along with these rights and freedoms have probably come certain responsibilities, such as doing chores, caring for younger siblings, keeping curfews, or following codes of conduct at school. Just as you have responsibilities that go along with your home or school rights, Canadian citizens also have responsibilities that go along with their citizenship.

It is very important to know both your rights and your responsibilities, because you cannot defend what you do not know exists. The best type of payment or reward is one that you feel you have earned, and fulfilling your responsibilities as a Canadian citizen is how you can feel that you have earned your rights.

Here are the responsibilities that Canada expects of its citizens:
- vote in elections
- help others in the community
- care for and protect our heritage (history and customs) and environment
- obey Canada's laws
- express opinions freely while respecting the rights and freedoms of others
- avoid discrimination, injustice, and unfairness

You demonstrate many of these responsibilities every day, often without even knowing it! Think about other ideas you could add to the web diagram that follows.

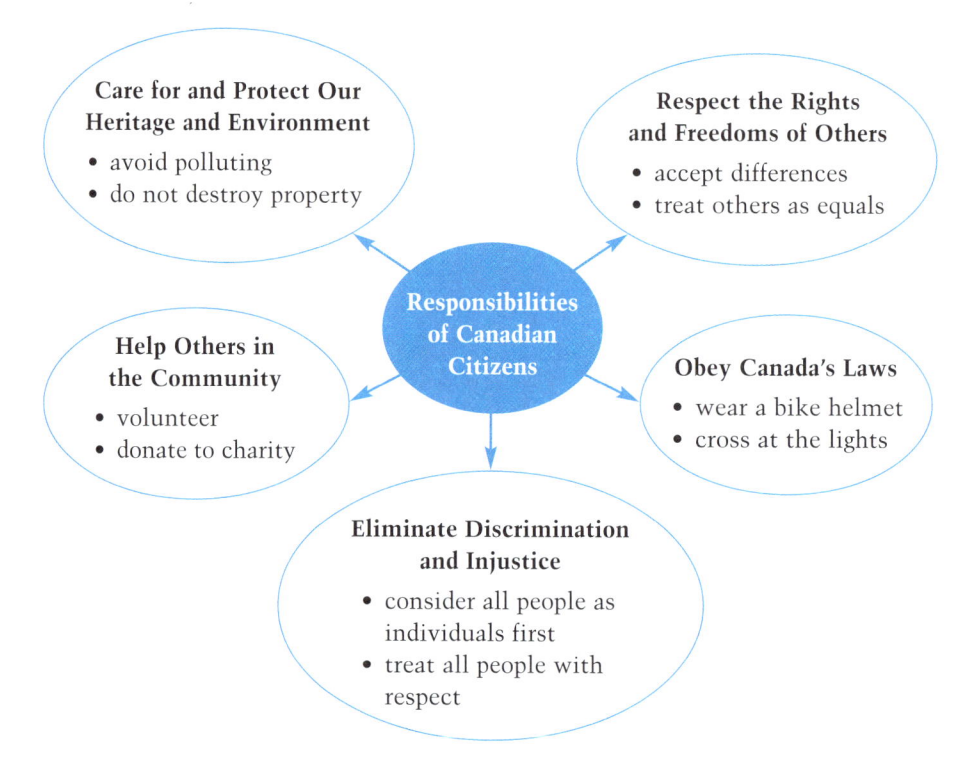

Responsibilities of Canadian Citizens

- **Care for and Protect Our Heritage and Environment**
  - avoid polluting
  - do not destroy property
- **Respect the Rights and Freedoms of Others**
  - accept differences
  - treat others as equals
- **Help Others in the Community**
  - volunteer
  - donate to charity
- **Obey Canada's Laws**
  - wear a bike helmet
  - cross at the lights
- **Eliminate Discrimination and Injustice**
  - consider all people as individuals first
  - treat all people with respect

CITIZEN IN ACTION

Tony Carella

Tony Carella and his family have been residents of Vaughan, a city north of Toronto, since 1982. After teaching history and law, working for a major Canadian corporation, and serving as a special assistant to a provincial cabinet minister, Carella decided to enter municipal politics. He has served as a city councillor in Vaughan for many years.

To strengthen the sense of community among residents and local businesses, Carella proposed the creation of a Declaration of Citizens' Rights and Responsibilities. It was approved by Vaughan city council in February 2005. Unlike the *Canadian Charter of Rights and Freedoms*, the declaration does not stand above the law but is intended to "teach people what rights citizenship gives them and what responsibilities it demands of them." The Declaration balances rights with responsibilities.

> **Every citizen has a right to**
> Live in a municipality that promotes community safety, health, and wellness, while safeguarding the natural environment.

Vaughan City Councillor Tony Carella (right) joins Vaughan Mayor Michael Di Biase (left) in presenting a Civic Hero Award to Bruno Dal Colle (centre). The Civic Hero Award is presented annually to one resident from each of the five local wards in recognition of outstanding civic responsibility.

Biography: A biography is an account of a person's life written by someone else. Like an autobiography, the writing is often vivid and personal in nature.

Every citizen has a responsibility to
Avoid behaviour that threatens the safety, health, and wellness of fellow citizens or the integrity of the natural environment

In a municipality, the responsibility mentioned above can be as simple as stopping at a stop sign. As Councillor Carella noted, "We have a terrible problem getting people to stop, really stop at stop signs… Our Declaration…is an attempt to remind our residents that they have responsibilities, like obeying stop signs."

Carella recommended distributing the Declaration to households, businesses, and elementary and secondary schools within Vaughan, and to other municipalities in Ontario. Although there is still much work to be done in publicizing the Declaration, Vaughan City Council adopted an awards program in 2005. Those who, on their own, do something that represents in an extraordinary way any of the responsibilities listed in the Declaration receive special recognition as "Civic Heroes."

Who are the civic heroes in your community? Choose one and write a brief biography about this person. File your biography in your Take Action Portfolio.

Exercising your rights and responsibilities is part of what it means to be a good citizen. History is filled with examples of people who took on the responsibility of righting a wrong, or making the world a better place. In a democratic society, there are many ways that citizens can take action and make a difference, either as individuals or as a group. They can write letters to political representatives or the local newspaper; organize protests, petitions, or boycotts; help fundraise for an important cause; vote in every election; participate in food drives; or visit seniors.

Often, the actions you take will be in response to other actions.

WHAT CAN YOU DO?

Work to End Gender Violence

On December 6, 1989, 14 female students at the École Polytechnique, the School of Engineering at the University of Montréal, were killed and 13 other students wounded by a single gunman intent on killing as many women as he could. He later killed himself. As he burst into a classroom, he fired two shots into the ceiling and shouted, "I want the women. I hate feminists!"

In response to these murders, Canadians and others around the world worked to remember the victims and condemn the anti-female anger of their attacker. The Canadian government has proclaimed

Rights and Responsibilities

A plaque on an exterior wall of École Polytechnique commemorates the 14 women killed during the Montréal massacre on December 6, 1989.

massacre: the merciless killing of large numbers of innocent people

December 6 as the National Day of Remembrance and Action on Violence Against Women. A variety of organizations across the country began the White Ribbon Movement in the early 1990s to remember the victims of the **massacre** (the merciless killing of large numbers of innocent people) and to protest against violence against women. The cause, supported by the white ribbon campaign, has now spread to a dozen countries around the world.

The Montréal Massacre was also an important step in the struggle for gun control in Canada. "It came right out of it," said Wendy Cukier, who founded the Coalition for Gun Control. This coalition would then go on to play a major part in lobbying Ottawa for laws that would ban all semi-automatic, military assault weapons and short-barrelled handguns, and require the registration of all firearms. The federal government responded to the concerns of women by introducing the gun registry. Although there have been concerns with respect to the cost of this initiative, most women's groups were satisfied with this response.

In September 2006, at Dawson College in Montréal, the random shooting of 19 students, and the death of one female student, highlighted the need for continued action toward gun control and against violence in society. As citizens, we all need to be aware of the extent to which some people in Canada use any licence to own firearms in a way that is dangerous to public safety. We need to be ready to participate in the debate over the firearms registry in Canada.

Passport to Civics

One of the international steps to fight global injustices is The 16 Days of Activism Against Gender Violence campaign (November 26 to December 10). This campaign was begun in 1991 arising from the first Women's Global Leadership Institute sponsored by the Center for Women's Global Leadership. These 16 days are selected because they include
- November 25, International Day Against Violence Against Women
- December 10, International Human Rights Day

These two dates thus link the idea that violence toward women is a violation of human rights. Other significant days that fall in this period are World Aids Day on December 1, and December 6, which marks the anniversary of the Montréal Massacre. They are the result of groups of average citizens taking action that leads to governments taking the bigger steps to make the world a safer place for all of us.

Identify three ways you might get involved in the campaign against gender violence.

The White Ribbon Campaign is the world's largest effort by men to end men's violence against women.

Rights and Responsibilities 81

APPLY YOUR LEARNING

1. a) Working with a partner, list five rights that you think would be very important to a municipality such as the city of Vaughan. Consider issues that exist in your community.
   b) Exchange your list with that of another pair group. Challenge them to develop a list of responsibilities that would balance each right.
2. Work with a small group to research the current status of the gun registry program in Canada. Find out what the responses of community organizations are, both for and against the plan. You may wish to search using the Coalition for Gun Control and the National Firearms Association for different perspectives on this issue.

CHAPTER 3 REVIEW

Build Vocabulary and Understanding

1. Take turns with a partner using each of the following words in a sentence. Provide feedback to your partner. Be sure to add the following words to your personal dictionary.
   a) rights
   b) freedoms
   c) discrimination
   d) judge
   e) jury
   f) court
   g) mediation
   h) arbitration
   i) *habeas corpus*
   j) laws
   k) youth justice
   l) responsibilities
   m) bias
   n) privacy

2. Identify the rights and responsibilities you have at home, at school, and in Canada. Why are there differences?

Think It Through

3. With a partner, find a newspaper article about a case involving youth crime.
   a) Working individually, summarize the case in your own words. Include the crime, name of the accused, date the crime was committed, and any witnesses. Determine what should happen to the accused if she or he is found guilty.
   b) Compare your thoughts with your partner.

4. Look at the list of rights and responsibilities you created in question 2. Identify which right and which responsibility is the most important to you. Explain why.

Share Your Voice

5. a) Research a situation involving privacy of information.
   b) Write a newspaper article about this situation. Remember to include the 5Ws+H (see pages 9 and 63) in the first paragraph. Include relevant quotations and details in the second and third paragraphs. Position the least relevant details in the last paragraphs.

Show You Care

6. Explain how your rights and responsibilities are connected with citizenship.

7. Research an example of a citizen's rights being restricted.
   a) What action did the individual take that led to the restriction of rights?
   b) What were the results of this case?
   c) Do you agree with the outcome? Explain.

Rights and Responsibilities

Take Action Portfolio

8. Review the notes you took during this chapter on what actions you would take to deal with your chosen issue if you had unlimited resources (money and time).
   a) Identify what should be done about the issue you have chosen. Consider brainstorming ideas with a small group, but record all the ideas discussed and include them in your Take Action Portfolio.
   b) List the steps you think should be taken. Number them in the order you think will work best.
   c) Beside each step, identify whom you would like to involve and why.
   d) Update your log with your progress so far.

CHAPTER 4

Rise and Resolution of Civic Conflict

After a rise in vicious dog attacks, the Ontario government banned pit bulls in 2005. It is now illegal to breed or bring pit bulls into the province. All existing pit bulls must be sterilized, and leashed and muzzled in public. But what is a pit bull? Many breeders, dog owners, even the Toronto Humane Society feel this law does very little to address the problem. What arguments might they have put forward? What could you suggest to solve the problem of vicious dog attacks?

Key Ideas
In this chapter, you will learn about
- *the causes of conflict*
- *some of the civic conflicts that have occurred in Canada*
- *ways conflicts are resolved in a democratic society*

TAP into Active Citizenship

As you work through this chapter, try to conduct more research on your issue to determine what is being done and by whom to resolve it. Keep a list of the organizations and people who are actively involved in this issue. What plan of action do they seem to be following? Think about what you can do to make a difference.

At the end of this chapter, you will create a realistic plan of action and follow this plan to make change. File all your notes in your Take Action Portfolio.

The Nature of Conflict

ACTIVATE YOUR THINKING

On a scale like the one below, rate your personal support for the following issues:

- *private health care*
- *freezing tuition fees (post-secondary school)*
- *banning use of pesticides and herbicides*
- *assisted suicide*
- *making panhandling illegal*
- *expanding nuclear energy production*
- *cancelling the gun registry*
- *stem-cell research*
- *anti-terrorism legislation*

1	2	3	4	5

Strongly oppose   **Neither oppose nor support**   **Strongly support**

Compare the results in a small group. Which issues caused the greatest debate? How might such disagreements be resolved?

Which issues do you think might cause the greatest amount of conflict in society? Discuss the possible reasons for such conflict. How might society resolve such conflicts?

Conflicts usually arise when there are differing points of view on an issue. The more points of view there are, or the more passionate people feel about the issue, the more difficult it is to resolve the conflict. Conflict can be very harmful if it is not resolved (fixed). Poor decisions, broken relationships, economic hardship, political instability, rights violations, even war can all result from unresolved conflict. This potential for disaster is why many organizations invest significant resources in researching the causes of, and possible solutions to, conflict. Their goal is to prevent conflict before it starts.

Public protests bring attention to issues that are sources of national conflict.

Passport to Civics

Causes of Conflict

At the root of all conflict, whether it is between individuals or groups, citizens and government, or nation versus nation, is difference. Our beliefs and values are shaped by the culture into which we are born. Personal experiences, age, gender, income, education, occupation, place of residence, friendships, and so on, affect our attitudes and points of view. They also affect how we respond to, and resolve, conflicts. When what we are trying to achieve meets with opposition from another source, conflict is the guaranteed result.

Conflicts can arise from economic differences, differences in beliefs and values, threats to rights and freedoms, or external causes.

Economic
- A co-worker is paid more per hour than you are for the same job

Beliefs and Values
- A vegetarian friend is angry with you for eating a hamburger

Rights, Freedoms, and Security
- You are bullied into shoplifting

External
- A rumour is started that you cheated on an exam

Usually the most serious types of conflict are caused by a combination of these four general causes. As you read the opposing viewpoints in the case studies that follow, try to identify which of the four causes of conflict is at the centre of each issue.

Women protest the killing of animals for their fur outside a US department store that sells furs.

CASE STUDY 22: FUR

Viewpoint A
"Today, the fur industry maintains a unique tradition and culture for thousands of Canadians who still live from the land. It plays an important role in environmental conservation and habitat management. [It] also contributes to international business and provides income for people in many rural and remote regions of Canada."
—The Fur Council of Canada

Viewpoint B
"Fur! It is very sad to see that in today's society certain cruel practices are so rampant and are still widely accepted. Amazingly, some people still actually think it is 'fashionable' to wear fur. Personally, I am embarrassed for anyone who wears fur, given the suffering caused to make the coats they buy."
—Anti-Fur Activist

Rise and Resolution of Civic Conflict

CASE STUDY 23: FORESTRY

Viewpoint A

"Citing current United Nations research, the complaint by the Suzuki Foundation, Greenpeace and Forest Ethics refutes claims by the Forest Products Association of Canada (FPAC) that Canada has the greatest amount of protected forest in the world, the most original remaining forest in the world, and that Canada's forests are expanding. United Nations research also shows that the integrity of Canada's forest ecosystems is at risk, and that Canada lags far behind other countries in terms of protecting its forests."
—David Suzuki Foundation

Viewpoint B

"The industry is committed to ensuring that Canada remains a world leader in sustainable forest management. Less than one quarter of one percent of our forests is harvested annually, and areas that are harvested are promptly regenerated. The industry operates under some of the toughest environmental laws and regulations in the world. Furthermore, Canada has become a world leader in the adoption of third-party certification, further ensuring sustainable forest management."
—Forest Products Association of Canada

CASE STUDY 24: CENSORSHIP

Viewpoint A

"Restrictions on freedom of speech have often drawn the CCLA's attention—from movie censorship to obscenity laws and banning of hate propaganda, to university speech codes and curtailment of picketing. In courts and legislative committees, the CCLA has fought for the right of Canadians to express themselves freely, even if the thoughts and opinions being expressed are offensive to most."
—Canadian Civil Liberties Association

Viewpoint B

The Ontario Film Review Board has been in existence since 1911. It was created because people in the province believed that the influence of moving images was so potentially powerful and pervasive that a censorship mechanism was needed to protect viewers—particularly young people—from harm.

Today, the Board's focus is classification, not censorship. The OFRB is a valued source of information about movies and videos that help viewers make the right entertainment decisions for themselves and for their children.

Therefore, the Ontario Film Review Board, through the *Theatres Act*, continues to limit access to films in those areas where there is a potential for harm to society, particularly to those who are most vulnerable.
—Ontario Film Review Board

APPLY YOUR LEARNING

1. a) Refer back to the web diagram on page 87. Think of one example from your personal life that you could you add to each of the four causes of conflict.

b) Complete an organizer like the one that follows for each of your examples.

Issue	Cause of Conflict	Resolved Yes or No	Outcome
Increase in allowance	Economic; Beliefs and Values: I felt I deserved an increase based on age, but my parents felt an increase should be earned.	Yes	In addition to my existing responsibilities, I agreed to take my brother and sister to the library once a week.
Wearing hats in school	Rights, Freedoms, and Security: I believe students should be able to wear what they want in school, as long as it is not offensive.	No	School board policy prohibits wearing headgear that is not for religious or safety reasons.

2. Choose an issue of civic importance that interests you.
   a) Find an article in a newspaper or on the Internet that appears to be in support of, or opposed to, a proposed solution to this issue.
   b) Identify the key arguments surrounding the issue. List them in point form in your notebook.
   c) Suggest an alternative solution to resolving the conflict. File a copy of the article and your notes in your Take Action Portfolio.

Conflict Resolution

ACTIVATE YOUR THINKING

Share with a partner a disagreement you have had and how you resolved it. As your partner shares his or her story, see if there are any similarities among the strategies that were used to resolve the conflict.

Our democratic society requires that we work to resolve conflicts in a fair and civilized manner. Often, this means all parties involved must accept a compromise (settle for less than what was originally wanted).

Strategies for Resolving Conflict

There are many approaches to resolving conflicts, whether they occur between you and your friends, or between citizens and the government. For these strategies to be successful, everyone involved must use them. Here are some examples:
- Active listening (not interrupting when others are speaking)
- Using "I" statements and affirmations, such as "I think I know what you mean by..." or "I felt the same way when..."

Anyone can create conflicts. It takes skill to resolve them. What strategies have you used to resolve conflicts in your own life?

Rise and Resolution of Civic Conflict

Idiomatic language: an idiom is a phrase or expression made up of two or more words. The meaning of the individual words cannot be combined to understand the meaning of the phrase. For example, the literal meaning of the two words in the idiom *middle ground* does not hint at the phrase's actual meaning, which is a position that is fair to both sides; a compromise. Idioms are understood by native speakers of a language.

- Recognizing types of responses to conflict that can lead to compromise (for example, responses that indicate both parties want the conflict to end and are willing to seek a resolution and find middle ground)
- Writing down what happened *before* discussing the conflict. This helps to keep the facts straight, releases emotional energy, and focuses attention on the main issue
- Asking closed questions, such as yes/no questions and questions that require specific, often short answers rather than explanations or opinions (for example, "On what day did this occur?" "Were you present?" "Who else was involved?")
- Practising the conflict mediation process so that the skills involved are easily applied when situations arise

In a democracy, it is important that individual citizens have the right and the opportunity to participate in the decision-making process that works to avert or resolve conflict. It is equally important that governments remain open and accountable to their citizens while making decisions and resolving conflicts in matters of civic importance.

Sometimes, however, people will say, "I don't care" when asked for their point of view. This reaction may mean the issue does not have a direct impact on them or their lives today. Or it may mean they feel no one is listening or they will have no influence on the decision-making process. But when many people express to their elected representatives the same point of view on an issue, those representatives often take action.

WHAT CAN YOU DO?

Volunteer

Resolving or reducing major conflicts affecting many citizens, thereby improving life for all of us, can be accomplished through two types of active citizenship: through involvement in the political process, and through non-political means, such as volunteering.

Volunteering not only helps you understand what your skills are and where they can best be used, but it also can help when it comes to applying for a job or for enrollment in college or university. Many potential employers and post-secondary institutions look favourably on applications that show evidence of active citizenship. Volunteer work can also contribute to the 40 hours of community service you are required to serve to graduate from high school in Ontario.

So, where can you get involved? Here are some suggestions:
- Check the guidance office at school for opportunities that may be posted. You might take part in activities that help new students feel welcome, or that help younger students to read.
- Support local, national, or international charities or organizations. These groups always need people to help make or put up signs, organize events, or help to raise funds. Even the smallest contribution can make a big difference.

Car washes are a great way for volunteers to raise funds for worthy causes.

Assessing websites for credibility: When using the Internet for research, be sure to check the website for accuracy and bias. Use these questions as a guide:
- Is the author or publisher of the website a credible expert?
- Is the website trying to sell something?
- Does the website contain accurate and up-to-date information?
- Is the information based on facts or opinions?
- Does the website credit sources of information? Double-check all sources of information against another credible source to ensure accuracy.

- Contact organizations that reflect and represent your interests. Perhaps there is a particular disease or condition for which you want to raise awareness. Contact their offices and begin to explore the possibilities.
- Visit the websites of reputable charitable or non-profit organizations (.org or .net) to find posted volunteer opportunities.
- Look around your community and in the telephone book to see what programs there are. Call and ask if they need help.
- Visit your city or town website. It may list volunteer opportunities in your community.
- Contact your local United Way, cultural arts association, student organization, or another association that can point you in the right direction.
- Find out if your library, place of worship, hospital, or community college sponsors any volunteer groups.

14 There are a multitude of opportunities to tap into in most communities, making it even easier to become an active citizen. It's up to you to decide how your personal beliefs and values fit into the needs of the community.

Discuss with a partner what you consider to be the advantages and disadvantages of being involved in a voluntary organization. Consider self-esteem, sense of empowerment, time commitment, the benefits of helping others, and so on.

15 Expressing your point of view may not be enough to resolve a conflict, however. Some disagreements require more action by citizens. Can you identify the conflict-resolution strategies in the headlines that follow?

Rise and Resolution of Civic Conflict

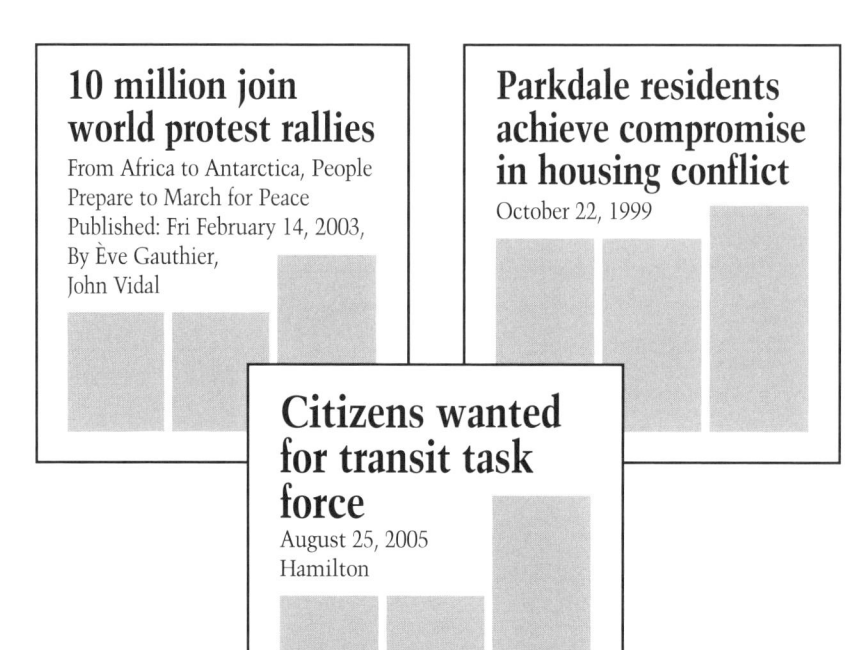

10 million join world protest rallies
From Africa to Antarctica, People Prepare to March for Peace
Published: Fri February 14, 2003,
By Ève Gauthier,
John Vidal

Parkdale residents achieve compromise in housing conflict
October 22, 1999

Citizens wanted for transit task force
August 25, 2005
Hamilton

Do we want to live in a neighbourhood with a main street like this:

...or like this:

Part of the campaign citizens launched to stop the drive-through included these visuals.

Often, elected representatives or civil servants will assemble all interested parties to discuss an issue of civic conflict. If more discussion is required, a commission of inquiry is set up. Occasionally, however, it becomes necessary for citizens to take more direct action on issues of importance to them personally.

As you read the following case study, identify the strategies the citizens used to stop a major corporation's plans to build a drive-through in their neighbourhood.

CASE STUDY 25: THE PEOPLE VS. MCDONALD'S

Citizens Beat Megacorp!
McDonald's Drops Court Challenge

"We do not intend to proceed with the existing legal action related to this situation," said Ron Christianson, corporate communications manager for McDonald's Restaurants of Canada.

As [City Councillor Joe] Mihevc said, "The conviction [firmness of belief] and persistence of the local residents' group was an inspirational tale. This agreement to dismiss on consent is their reward. Toronto is a safer city for pedestrians and for local communities. St. Clair West in particular is a better place for small business to operate, and our communities can continue to flourish unhindered by inappropriate drive-thru developments."

On January 23, 2004, McDonald's and other representatives of the drive-through industries lost their appeal to the Ontario Municipal Board of the city-wide bylaw that prohibits the construction of drive-throughs 30 metres from residential properties.

Passport to Civics

As you read the following press release from the province of Nova Scotia, consider the strategies governments use to resolve issues. In what ways are they similar to or different from the methods individuals use?

CASE STUDY 26: GOVERNMENT APPROACH TO RESOLVING CONFLICTS

Conference Builds on Success
Premier's Office
August 29, 2005 18:23

The ties between eastern Canada and New England were further strengthened today, August 29, by a number of innovative regional initiatives, said Premier John Hamm.

Premier Hamm said this year's Conference of New England Governors and Eastern Canadian Premiers focused on trade relations, the environment, security, and energy issues.

"Nova Scotians know how important these relationships are in building our prosperity," said the premier. "When we co-operate on major issues like protecting our environment and increasing investment and trade, everyone benefits."

CITIZEN IN ACTION

Richard Mewhinney

When it comes to active citizenship, the best place to start is at the grassroots' level—in your own community. Newmarket, Ontario, resident Richard Mewhinney did just that. It is not unusual for him to spend 10 to 20 hours a week involved in community activities.
- As a teen in the late 1970s, he got involved in organizations such as the Boy Scouts, in high school activities, and in church groups.
- He became Director at Large of Neighbourhood Heart of York, a group that assembles volunteers from various member churches to help those less fortunate gain access to much-needed resources.

Rise and Resolution of Civic Conflict

- He is a member of a number of local committees, such as *Newmarket Vote 2006 Task Force*. This committee is working to evaluate the causes of low voter turnout in municipal elections and to recommend strategies to improve citizen involvement.
- He serves as a director for *INN from the Cold*. This initiative provides shelter during the cold winter months for homeless people in the community. The warming centre, which is open on nights when the temperature falls below –15°C, is staffed by volunteers, including town employees.

Richard Mewhinney's philosophy of active citizenship is simple.

"My ultimate goal is to try to leave this world/community better than when I came.... I find that when people expect that everything will be done for them, they all too often are disappointed with the result. I prefer to ask "How can I make things better?" I have come to realize that there are many people who are asking the same question, and that's how active citizens both get the work done and enjoy the process."

Write a brief autobiographical profile. Identify a core value or belief you hold. State where you think you could make the greatest contribution to your community or the world, either now or in the future.

In July 2005, Richard Mewhinney (right) was awarded a Community Volunteer Ambassador medal during a ceremony honouring 125 of Newmarket's most active citizens. "The medal was a great honour," he says, "but the feeling that a person has made a small difference in the place where he lives is the real reward."

APPLY YOUR LEARNING

---

1. a) What methods do citizens use to resolve conflict?
   b) Work with a small group to prepare a role play in which you try to resolve an issue affecting your school or community.
2. Choose an issue from this chapter that you feel strongly about, or come up with another one that is important to you. Write a letter to the editor expressing your point of view. Explain what you think should be done to resolve the problem. You may want to do some research first to find out the various points of view on the issue and what steps have already been taken to reach a solution.

Conflicts with Government

ACTIVATE YOUR THINKING

What issues seem to be causing conflict between government and the public today? Think about what you have heard recently on television or read in the newspaper. Try to list at least three of these conflict issues in your notebook. Circle the one that is most important to you personally.

Just as you can become involved in conflict on a personal level, conflicts can also develop with various levels of government. Sometimes politicians disagree about what action should be taken to solve a problem. Sometimes different groups disagree over the decisions made by politicians or other groups. Stories of these types of civic conflicts fill our newspapers almost every day.

Examples include questions of whether government should increase taxes to provide more services or lower taxes and reduce services. Most people want lower taxes *and* more services, but this is no more possible than your being able to spend the *same* $50 on a new outfit and a new video game.

Another example is whether communities should have casinos. On the one hand, casinos create jobs for local people, but these benefits come at the cost of people who become addicted to gambling, and this causes problems for their families. Others have argued that the presence of casinos can lead to a high rate of crime for the community. These types of issues cause civic conflict as citizens and politicians try to come to an agreement about what to do.

Many Canadians do not realize that the government is always looking for citizen input. Citizens can become very involved at the municipal level, where government influence on day-to-day life is most closely felt. Joining municipal committees, boards, and organizations is a good way to have a voice in the decisions that directly affect you.

Aboriginal Peoples and Civic Conflict

Have you ever done something wrong without really understanding why it was wrong until you became more mature? Just as it can happen to you, it can happen to governments. After all, governments do represent and reflect the beliefs and values of the people or society they represent. In the case of Aboriginal peoples living in Canada (First Nations, Inuit, and Métis), there is a long history of governments not doing the right thing.

Land claims is one major area of conflict that is ongoing. This issue can be traced back to the arrival of Europeans on North American soil beginning in the 15th century. European explorers claimed vast amounts of land on behalf of a foreign country or monarch. The land they claimed was not without inhabitants, however. Aboriginal peoples, who were the original occupiers of the region before the Europeans arrived, had a clear claim to the land, even though they did not believe in ownership of land in the European sense.

Over the next 500 years different North American governments made arrangements with numerous Aboriginal groups, such as restricting where Aboriginal peoples could live. Rarely could these arrangements be considered fair. Although our understanding of what is fair changes as the beliefs and values of society change, conflicts still arise when it comes to limited resources such as land.

What message is the picture above sending? What evidence do you have for this? Who is the message targeting? Why?

Rise and Resolution of Civic Conflict

Cutting down old growth forests threatens the land-based culture of many Aboriginal peoples.

When the *Charter of Rights and Freedoms* was signed into law in 1982, section 25 dealt specifically with Aboriginal rights. The intent was to allow Aboriginal groups to continue to argue for traditional land rights, often in courts of law.

> 25. The guarantee in this Charter of certain rights and freedoms shall not be construed [interpreted or understood] so as to abrogate [put an end to] or derogate [undermine] from any aboriginal treaty or other rights or freedoms that pertain to the aboriginal peoples of Canada including
> a) any rights or freedoms that have been recognized by the Royal Proclamation of October 7, 1763; and
> b) any rights or freedoms that now exist by way of land claims agreements or may be so acquired.

In recent years, a number of events have made headlines across the country and around the world on the issue of Aboriginal land claims. As you read about these different events in the pages that follow, use a graphic organizer like the one below to help you track the viewpoints, beliefs, and actions involved.

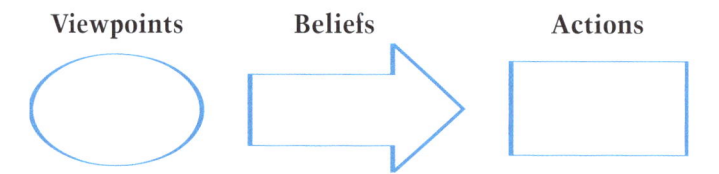

Viewpoints → **Beliefs** → **Actions**

The Oka Crisis

In July 1990, the Mohawks of Kanesatake (Oka) objected when the municipality planned to expand a golf course over ancient Mohawk burial grounds. When this conflict could not be resolved, the Mohawks set up barricades. The conflict grew as the Sûreté du Québec (provincial police) were called in and set up their own barricades. Gunfire erupted, as a result of which a police officer died. The Canadian Army was then called in to deal with the situation and the protest reached a new level.

An armed standoff between the Mohawks and the army lasted for 78 days. Suddenly, the world was made aware of the issues of Aboriginal rights and land claims. Tensions grew within the Mohawk community and the town of Oka, as the conflict made many people feel like hostages or prisoners in their own homes.

Both sides were negotiating over a number of issues related to land and control of community services, such as policing and education. The standoff ended on September 26 when the barricades were removed. The main objectives of the Mohawks had been met. The federal government purchased the proposed golf course lands and released them to Kanesatake.

The Oka crisis was an example of a First Nations community working together to protect traditional rights. Here, young and old celebrate in 2000, the 10th anniversary of the Oka crisis.

A number of positive changes occurred as a result of this conflict. The first involved the governing system of the Mohawks. There had been problems within the Mohawk community in terms of how the leadership was determined. Before the crisis, Clan Mothers elected three chiefs from each of the Turtle, Bear, and Wolf clans. This hereditary system created eight chiefs and a Grand Chief of the Mohawk Council of Kanesatake. After the crisis, a different system was established. Every community member had the right to vote. The number of chiefs to be elected was reduced to six, with the Grand Chief also being elected by the people. A Mohawk police force was established to replace the Sûreté du Québec. A number of residences and public buildings, such as a police station, health centre, and Elders' home were built, and roads were improved.

Sites in eastern Canada of recent land-claim disputes

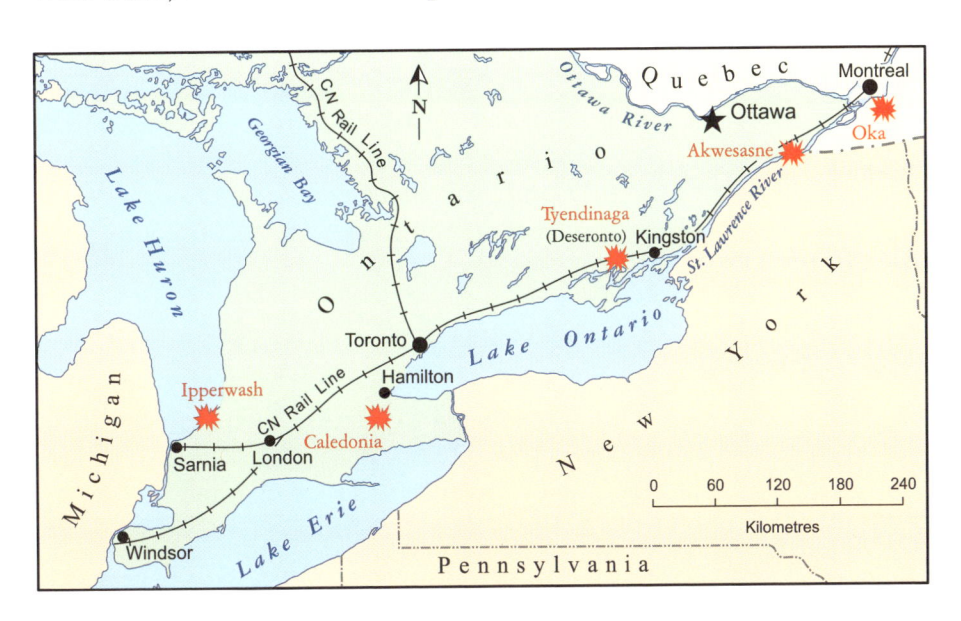

Rise and Resolution of Civic Conflict 97

The death of Dudley George (pictured here in 1993) sparked a public inquiry. It had been over 100 years since a land-rights dispute in Canada had ended in the death of an Aboriginal person.

Ipperwash

Five years after Oka, a group of 30 Anishinabe from the Stony Point First Nations staged a protest in Ipperwash Provincial Park, located on the south shore of Lake Huron. This particular protest was a continuation of a dispute that began in 1942, during World War II. The dispute was over land that the Canadian Army had taken in that year to set up a temporary military training camp. The Anishinabe claimed this land as a sacred burial ground.

Although the government had paid some compensation to the Anishinabe over the years, no effort was made to return the land that had been taken decades earlier.

On the evening of September 6, 1995, Anthony (Dudley) George was among approximately 30 people who peacefully occupied Ipperwash Provincial Park to protest the destruction of their sacred burial ground. Although reports as to whether the protesters were armed differed at first, the Ontario Provincial Police (OPP) opened fire and an unarmed Dudley George was killed. The officer responsible was convicted of criminal negligence causing death. He resigned from the force.

The family of Dudley George suspected that the provincial government at the time had had something to do with the actions taken by the OPP. They campaigned for several years for a public inquiry to be held into George's death and were finally granted one. The commission of inquiry began in July 2004 and ended in August 2006. The report, which contained findings and recommendations aimed at preventing violence in similar circumstances, was made public on May 31, 2007.

Although public inquiries are set up to investigate and report on matters that have a significant amount of public interest and are paid for by the government, the commission is independent. The goal is to ensure that, in future, such wrongs are never repeated. All provincial ministries and agencies are required to co-operate with the commission. Except in some matters of public security, the testimony delivered at the hearings is public, and the proceedings are published.

In his report, Judge Sidney Linden concluded that treaties that were signed perhaps hundreds of years ago are not "relics of the past" but "living agreements" that must be respected by all Ontarians. He went on to say that everything Ontarians enjoy resulted from treaties that were often negotiated to the supreme disadvantage of Aboriginal peoples.

Caledonia

Even as the Ipperwash Inquiry was proceeding in April 2006, another major confrontation developed in Caledonia, just west of Toronto. Here, the Six Nations set up blockades to stop the building of a subdivision on land they claimed was illegally taken away from them 200 years ago. The provincial negotiator in the case, who was appointed by the Ontario premier, said it was crucial for the Caledonia dispute to be ended responsibly, because Aboriginal peoples across North America were watching. "Don't underestimate the significance," he warned. "All of us were praying and working hard to ensure that something ugly didn't develop out of this...."

As you read the following case study, try to identify the similarities and differences between this situation and the events at Oka, Ipperwash, and Caledonia.

CASE STUDY 27: RAIL LINE BLOCKADE

Native protesters block Ontario's main rail line

The Canadian Press
DESERONTO, Ont. (Apr 21, 2007)

Aboriginal protesters vowed yesterday to maintain their planned 48-hour blockade of eastern Ontario's main rail corridor despite a court injunction ordering them off the railway crossing.

The tense situation prompted Ontario Premier Dalton McGuinty to urge the federal government to intervene at the "earliest possible opportunity."

The long-simmering land dispute near Deseronto, Ontario, erupted around midnight Thursday as members of the Mohawks of the Bay of Quinte moved to block the rail line, shutting down freight and passenger train service from Toronto eastward to Ottawa and Montreal.

Natives are protesting a developer's plan to build condominiums using material from a quarry on land they claim is theirs.

Protest organizer Shawn Brant accepted a copy of the injunction and shook the hand of the police officer who read the court order to the protesters at the site, some 30 kilometres west of Kingston. Brant said they'll leave peacefully after 48 hours, but not before.

Why do you think the premier would ask the federal government to intervene in this protest?

Rise and Resolution of Civic Conflict 99

Conflicts arising from treaties that were signed hundreds of years ago continue to require resolution today. Closely linked to these land-claims conflicts is the issue of Aboriginal self-government. This is another major area where there are conflicting opinions and contrasting civic purposes.

CITIZENS IN ACTION

Inuit Circumpolar Council (ICC)

The Inuit Circumpolar Council was founded in 1977. It represents 160 000 Inuit from Canada, Alaska (USA), Greenland, and Chukotka (Russia), and holds consultative status at the United Nations. Inuit believed that to grow in their circumpolar homeland, they needed to speak with a united voice and work together to protect and promote their way of life.

The ICC General Assembly is held every four years, at which time a new leadership is elected and cultural bonds are strengthened. The goals of the ICC include

- to strengthen unity among Inuit of the circumpolar region
- to promote Inuit rights and interests on an international level
- to develop and encourage long-term policies that safeguard the Arctic environment
- to seek full and active partnership in the political, economic, and social development of circumpolar regions

What strategies for change are Inuit using to protect and promote their interests? Which of these strategies could you use in your action plan for change? Explain.

The ICC logo features the Inuit drum. In addition to being a musical instrument, the Inuit drum represents unity and tolerance. The earth tone of the logo symbolizes harmony with the environment.

Aboriginal Self-Governance

Both Oka and Ipperwash, and now Caledonia and Deseronto, have sparked further examination of the need for Aboriginal self-government. Many First Nations object to the government of Canada setting the rules about how their government should function. Note the arguments put forth by the Anishinaabeg Nation communities in the case study that follows.

CASE STUDY 28: NEGOTIATING ON AN EQUAL FOOTING

No! To Self-Government Initiative
Citizens Reject United Anishinaabeg Councils' Agreement with Canada

Four Anishinaabeg Nation communities in Central Ontario voted against what would have been the first self-government agreement in Canada outside of a comprehensive land claim or treaty. The deal would have included a regional form of government. As Grand Council Chief John

Grand Council Chief John Beaucage of the Anishinaabeg Nation

100   *Passport to Civics*

Beaucage explained, "The rejection of this agreement is not so much a rejection of self-government, but more of a rejection of the federal government's concept of negotiating. We have inherent [natural] rights that are granted by the Creator, not by the Minister or by the Indian Act. These cannot be limited by government policy."

On April 1, 1999, Inuit gained self-rule and control over their land with the birth of the new territory of Nunavut. Numerous debates and votes, called *plebiscites*, involving the largely Inuit population of the Northwest Territories, preceded this historic event.

Interior of the Nunavut legislature, the seat of government

APPLY YOUR LEARNING

1. Based on the situations you have read about in this section, which conflict resolution strategies do you think are effective? Which do you think are ineffective? Explain your reasoning to a partner.
2. Create a Venn diagram comparing the similarities and differences between the Oka Crisis and Ipperwash. Consider the causes, the events, the people and governments involved, and the resolution.
3. List the ways a public inquiry might help to resolve future conflicts. Consider researching the inquiries into Ipperwash, the water crisis in Walkerton, Ontario, or the Air India disaster to help you formulate your ideas.
4. Continue this T-chart in your notebook, adding reasons why Aboriginal peoples in Canada might wish to govern themselves and why others might be opposed.

For Aboriginal Self-Government	Against Aboriginal Self-Government
• opportunity to preserve traditional culture • ensure historical agreements are honoured	• the country runs more smoothly when everyone is bound by the same laws under one government

Rise and Resolution of Civic Conflict

Environmental Conflicts

ACTIVATE YOUR THINKING

environment: the quality of the air, water and land in or on which people, animals and plants live

*Create a mind map in your notebook for the word **environment**. List as many ideas and images as you can related to this topic. Add your ideas to a class mind map. Take a poll to determine which aspect of the environment is of concern to most people in your class. Discuss why this issue might be so important to so many people.*

Global warming, species extinction, genetically engineered foods, deforestation, water quality, noise pollution, waste management, pesticides. Clearly, humans have a very significant—and not always positive—impact on Earth. Few issues involve so many people and generate as much heated debate as issues related to the environment. It is a major source of conflict in our world.

CITIZEN IN ACTION

Simon Jackson

When he was 13, British Columbia student Simon Jackson heard about North America's rarest bear, the white Kermode, or spirit bear, and the plans to develop its habitat. He knew he had to help. The Kermode bear is a unique subspecies of the black bear, found only on Canada's west coast, and numbers less than 400. Jackson founded The Spirit Bear Youth Coalition, an all youth-run organization to create a new type of environmental advocacy group.

In April 2001, at the age of 18, Jackson's Youth Coalition helped create a historic land-use agreement. It was the largest land protection measure in North American history. Logging companies, First Nations, all levels of government, and environmental groups agreed to a framework for sustainability on the west coast. The agreement also helped to protect half of the spirit bear's last intact habitat and delay development of the other half.

> *"When I embarked on this campaign...I began by looking through a phone book and contacting everyone I thought might have some insight on this issue—and the more I learned from all sides, the more I realized how badly this bear needed a voice. I felt the best chance I had at uniting people to help save the spirit bear was the group I was able to relate to most closely—my peers. I stuttered my way through speeches to every English class in my school and by the end of the day, I collected 700 letters to mail to then-BC Premier Glen Clark, in support of saving the spirit bear. But when a form letter came to me in the mail a few months later, I realized that it would take a lot more to save the bears.*

Simon Jackson

When I founded the Spirit Bear Youth Coalition, it was one of the first all youth-run organizations in Canada and the first involved in this issue. Although at first I felt young people would be the only demographic [population group] I would be able to mobilize for the spirit bear, I began to realize that engaging young people, in and of itself, was critical. Too often decisions are made that directly affect the future of today's youth...without any input from youth. As important as it was to give the spirit bear a strong voice at the decision making table, it was equally important to have meaningful representation from young people at the decision making table—to give young people hope, to capture their imagination, and to provide new insight on long staled issues. The Youth Coalition continues to prove that when any young persons, from any walk of life, stand up and are counted on the issues they care about, they can make a difference for all life. It is this achievement that gives me the most pride...."

Jackson was honoured as one of *Time Magazine*'s Heroes for the Planet. Today, the Spirit Bear Youth Coalition has over 6 million young people involved in 65 countries.

Simon Jackson believes in the power of one, that anyone with a loud enough voice can make a difference. Do you agree? Explain.

Air Pollution

Did you know that in the middle of winter Canadians idle their cars for a combined total of over 75 million minutes a day? That is equal to one car idling for 144 years. Why? Because the belief is that it helps the car warm up faster. Canadians use that reason in the winter as well as in the summer, when air conditioning applies!

How are these two messages similar? Which do you think is more effective? Why?

PSA: a public service announcement (PSA) is a non-commercial advertisement created to inform or educate the public about a specific issue. PSAs are usually broadcast on radio or television, but sometimes take the form of poster campaigns.

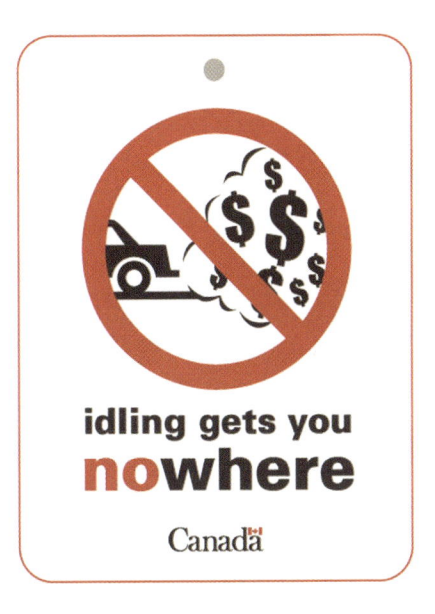

Rise and Resolution of Civic Conflict 103

What is the message of this cartoon?

Pollution from an idling vehicle is only one of many types of pollution we face. According to the Toronto Public Health Department, cars are the largest source of harmful air pollutants. It estimates that air pollution in Toronto alone is connected with 1000 early deaths and 5500 hospital visits every year!

During the hot summer months in Ontario, you may hear information about the Air Quality Index or reports of a smog advisory. Smog (a combination of the words *smoke* and *fog*) is a major type of pollution. Where does smog come from? It comes from many chemical sources, including the following:
- gas and diesel-powered cars, trucks, buses, boats, and lawnmowers
- factories and industrial processes
- oil-based paints, cleaners, and other solvents
- pesticides and herbicides
- road paving and other construction activities

Pollution is the responsibility of all three levels of government for obvious reasons. But disagreements often arise as to which level of government is in charge of what and who should pay for what. Sometimes, areas of legal authority and the willingness to cover the cost of making changes conflict. For example, to expand public transit, which is a municipal responsibility, there is an expectation that the federal and provincial governments should help. In the case of pesticides, municipalities can restrict the use of these chemicals within their boundaries, but they cannot stop the sale of them. This is a provincial responsibility.

Many people are concerned about the health risks posed by the use of pesticides and herbicides. A report by the Ontario College of Family Physicians identified pesticides as being associated with cancer and reproductive problems. Organizations such as the Canadian Cancer Society and the Registered Nurses Association of Ontario share these concerns. Others, however, argue that the amount of pesticides used by homeowners is very small and does not pose a health concern. They also argue that using the chemicals helps to lessen the symptoms of allergy sufferers, and helps to prevent some invasive species from destroying the habitats of other species.

To resolve environmental issues requires the co-operation of governments and individuals. It is not enough to rely on others to do the right thing. We all must take responsibility. As you read the following list of ways to resolve the pollution problem, think about who would support these ideas, who would oppose them, and why.
- increase public transit
- limit access to cities, allowing entry to public transit vehicles, bicycles, and foot traffic only
- make hybrid vehicles cheaper
- reduce coal-burning electricity
- plant trees to create shade and reduce the need for air conditioning

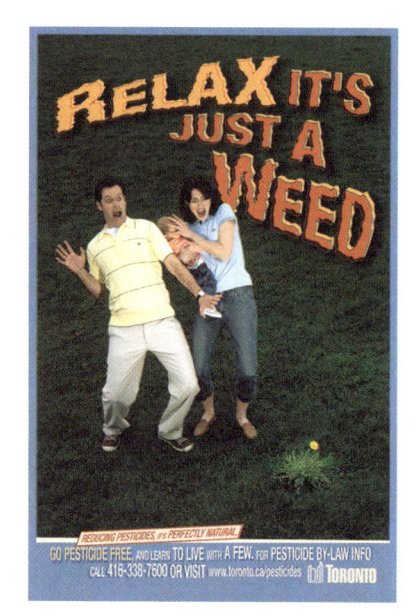

The City of Toronto launched its 2004 ban on pesticide use with a poster campaign.

- don't pave parking areas
- lower temperatures in winter and raise temperatures in summer in homes, offices, and malls
- turn off electrical appliances when not in use, even for short periods of time
- walk more (or use a bicycle)
- build more bicycle lanes
- plant roof gardens ("green roofs") on flat-roofed buildings
- develop more self-sustaining communities, where people can live, work, access essential services, and spend leisure time
- invest in alternative energy sources (wind, solar, biomass)

APPLY YOUR LEARNING

1. Write a letter to one level of government (your MP, MPP, or municipal councillor), asking them what they are doing to help reduce pollution. Present your ideas of what they should be doing to the entire class or a small group.
2. Do you think the municipality that bans pesticide use cares more for its citizens than the municipality that doesn't? Debate this issue in small groups.

Waste Management

ACTIVATE YOUR THINKING

Working with a partner, recall an item you recently threw out. Where did you put it? Why? What do you think will happen to it next? Try to predict the final destination of your item, and the steps it took to get there.

Garbage is not a topic many people like to think about. But do you know where your garbage ends up after you put it in a container?

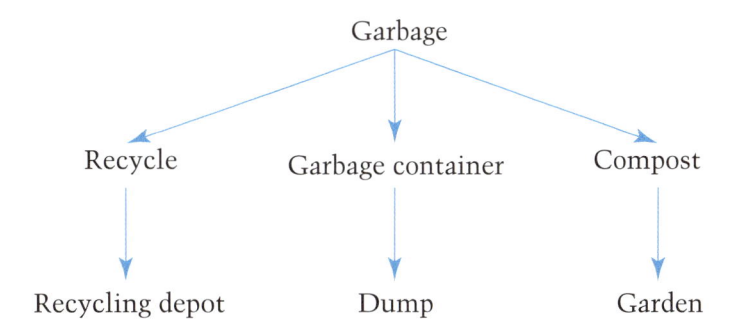

```
                    Garbage
                   /   |   \
                  /    |    \
            Recycle  Garbage  Compost
                    container
               |       |        |
               ↓       ↓        ↓
         Recycling    Dump    Garden
           depot
```

Our garbage affects the quality of the air we breathe. The garbage that is decomposing in our landfill sites is creating methane gas, which is one of many greenhouse gases. With most North Americans generating about two kilograms of garbage per day, it's no wonder we have an air quality problem.

The question of what to do with garbage has been a hot topic in many communities. In recent years, some Ontario cities have been grappling with the garbage problem. Local landfills were reaching capacity and had to be closed. Solutions were sought and several cities, including Toronto, chose to truck their garbage to the United States, where the state of Michigan was willing to dispose of it for a fee. Not surprisingly, the people of Michigan were not happy with this plan.

The NIMBY effect (Not in My Backyard) is a major obstacle in many civic conflicts. After all, who wants convicted sex offenders living in halfway houses in their neighbourhood? Who wants homeless people sleeping on benches in their park? Who wants other people's garbage landing on their doorstep?

One plan that Toronto had in the 1990s was to send its garbage to an empty mine in Northern Ontario, near Kirkland Lake and Englehart. Toronto City Council thought this was a great plan, as the garbage would be gone from Toronto. The government of Ontario thought that it was a good idea, too, even changing some laws to speed up the approval process. A company named Rail Cycle North had a plan to transport the garbage to the abandoned Adams Mine in Kirkland Lake.

Some people in the Kirkland Lake area also liked the idea, as it would create many jobs in an area that had high unemployment. However, there were also many people in the Kirkland Lake area who were opposed to this plan. They were worried about the environmental impact of garbage put into the ground and the potential risks involved if it entered the water system.

As you read the following case study, use a graphic organizer like the one below to help you record information and ideas. Try to include in your notes the arguments against sending Toronto's garbage to Kirkland Lake. Also identify how supporters of the proposed solution might have countered each of the arguments.

What message does this sign send? Who is it targeting?

Symbols/signs: signs often use simple pictures that are stereotypes as short and effective ways of getting a message across to the reader. If these signs are very successful so that many people identify one idea, person, company, or organization with one graphic image, it becomes a symbol.

It says... (evidence from the text)	I say... (my reaction to this point)	And so... (conclusions I can draw)

CASE STUDY 29: ADAMS MINE

Dr. Richard Denton was elected mayor of Kirkland Lake in 1997, based on his concerns about the shipment of Toronto's garbage. He worked long hours to change the minds of the Ontario government, the members of Toronto City Council, as well as the people in his own community who were in favour of this plan. In September, 2000, just before the municipal election, he spoke at a rally and said, "The people of Toronto should ask three questions. Is this the best solution for the environment? Is this the best deal for TO [Toronto]? Are we sending it to a willing host?"

Dr. Denton also noted that the "garbage plan is a negative thing because the Rail Cycle North deal needs one million tons of garbage to be financially viable [workable]. This means Toronto will have an incentive not to divert [change existing ways], reuse and recycle." Dr. Denton believed that not only was transporting Toronto's garbage bad for the environment, but it would also be a disaster for tourism and would, as well, make it difficult for Kirkland Lake to recruit new doctors to the town.

62 In October 2000, the Timiskaming First Nation took a strong position against the Adams Mine proposal, organizing a rail-line blockade near the small town of Earlton. Many local people who were also opposed to the plan joined in the protest. Local businessman Pierre Belanger became the spokesperson for Against the Adams Mine Campaign. That same year, members of the Timiskaming First Nation and members of the Against the Adams Mine Campaign went to Switzerland to express their opposition to Toronto winning the 2008 Olympic Games, because Toronto's plan was environmentally unsound. Toronto did not win the Olympic bid.

63 Despite seemingly overwhelming support for the anti-Adams Mine side, Mayor Denton lost the municipal election in 2000. The people of Kirkland Lake chose to use the mine for Toronto's garbage. Opposition remained strong, however, with one member of the anti-mine campaign stating, "There are 21 municipalities in this region adamantly opposed to the development of this dump. Anyone looking to test the so-called 'willingness' of Temiskaming will face more demonstration, blockades, and a campaign that can now count on national support."

64 In January 2004, the Liberal government passed legislation that ended consideration of Adams Mine as a site for Toronto's garbage. Although this move resolved the issue for the people of Kirkland Lake and northern Ontario, the problem of where to dispose of Toronto's garbage remained. The issue also generated widespread awareness of the need to find better ways of dealing with waste.

65 After considerable public debate and with a notice from the state of Michigan that it was cancelling its agreement to accept garbage from Ontario, a new plan was required. In October 2006, Toronto Mayor David Miller announced that the city had purchased the Green Lane Landfill in St. Thomas, Ontario. The purchase resolved the problem temporarily by providing Toronto with a site that had already been approved for landfill in a Canadian community. However, Toronto continues to search for a more permanent solution.

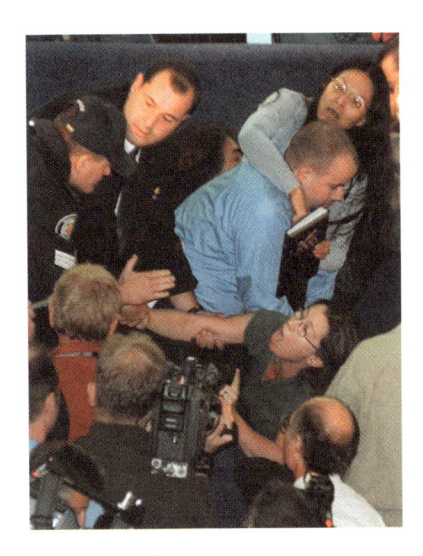

What message do these pictures send? Which method of conflict resolution do you think is more effective? Why?

Aboriginal place names: Canadians borrow many place names from Aboriginal languages. *Canada* comes from the Huron word *Kanata*, meaning "settlement" or "village." *Ontario* comes from the Huron language as well. It was first applied to the lake, but may be a corruption of *onitariio*, meaning "beautiful lake," or *kanadario*, which translates as "sparkling" or "beautiful" water.

APPLY YOUR LEARNING

1. Discuss with a partner whether the provincial government's decision to deny local voters in northern Ontario the option of accepting Toronto's garbage was justified.

Rise and Resolution of Civic Conflict

2. Prepare a 'Both Sides' organizer as follows. Determine where the following points would go, and then add some of your own:
   - not enough room within the city borders
   - the city produces so much garbage and is therefore responsible for disposing of it
   - it's an incentive to be more environmentally aware of our limited resources
   - it provides jobs for smaller communities with less economic opportunities
   - every community should just incinerate (burn) its own garbage

Evidence That Supports	Issue	Evidence That Opposes
	Every city should deal with its own garbage in its own community	

Decision

Reasons

3. Find out what your school does with its garbage.
   a) First, determine what types of garbage the school has to deal with (for example, paper waste, hazardous waste such as paint cans and batteries, and food waste).
   b) Next, identify what types of alternative waste-management solutions it follows or promotes (for example, garbage-free lunches, recycling, composting, donating). If your school has an environmental club, find out what priorities or goals it has for reducing school waste.
   c) Then research some ways your school could further reduce its contribution to your local landfill site.
   d) Finally, create a Waste Awareness campaign (posters, announcements over the PA system, school newsletter article) that encourages everyone to work together to solve the garbage problem.

CHAPTER 4 REVIEW

Build Vocabulary and Understanding

1. Define each of the following words, then create a picture or image for each one that will help you understand the concept. Stick figures are acceptable. Be sure the words are added to your personal dictionary.
   - a) conflict
   - b) Aboriginal peoples
   - c) land claims
   - d) self-government
   - e) blockade
   - f) public inquiry
   - g) pollution
   - h) unemployment
   - i) task force
   - j) resolution
   - k) NIMBY
   - l) incinerate

2. a) Working with a partner, take five minutes to prepare a brief oral presentation on one of the words in question 1 that you find most interesting. Your presentation must explain what the word means. Be sure you have a good understanding of the word, as you will not be able to read your presentation. Use examples to help you explain the concept. Practise with your partner.

   b) Create a word web showing some of the related words. Post your web in the classroom after your presentation.

Think It Through

3. Reread Case Studies 25 through 29 in this chapter. Create a chart like the one below. For each case study, identify
   - the issue
   - the beliefs and values involved
   - the approach used to resolve the conflict
   - what you would have done to try and resolve the conflict as (i) a citizen, and (ii) a government official

Issue	Beliefs and Values	Approach Used	What I Would Have Done
			Citizen: Government Official:
			Citizen: Government Official:

Rise and Resolution of Civic Conflict

Share Your Voice

4. a) Working with a partner, debate this statement: "Civic conflicts can always be resolved peacefully." Use the following process, called Timed Retell, for this activity.
   - Step 1: Partner A presents his or her point of view for one minute, while Partner B listens
   - Step 2: Partner B retells Partner A's point of view
   - Step 3: Partner B shares his or her point of view for one minute, while Partner A listens
   - Step 4: Partner A retells Partner B's point of view

   b) Write a letter to the editor using evidence from the other partner!

Show You Care

5. Create a poster to demonstrate one of the following: how to resolve a conflict, how to reduce smog, or ways to volunteer.
   a) Once you have chosen your topic, plan the key message, and then prepare a draft of your poster.
   b) Obtain feedback from two or three classmates on your draft poster before you finalize it.

Take Action Portfolio

6. You now have an issue that requires some action to make change.
   a) Research more on this topic. Use at least three different sources, such as newspaper articles, interviews, and the Internet.
   b) Make notes as you research. File these in your Take Action Portfolio. They will provide the background information for your final report.
   c) Create your plan of action. What steps will you take to achieve your goal? Review the ideas in this book. Focus on the strategies others have used that seemed to be successful.
   d) Take action now! Write letters, make a poster, organize a fund-raising campaign, prepare a petition to be sent to a key individual, start a newsletter. If you are working with others, divide up the tasks so that each group member is responsible for completing one part of the action plan.
   e) Continue to update your log with your thoughts regarding the progress you have made. Be sure you file everything in your Take Action Portfolio.

CHAPTER 5
Global Citizenship

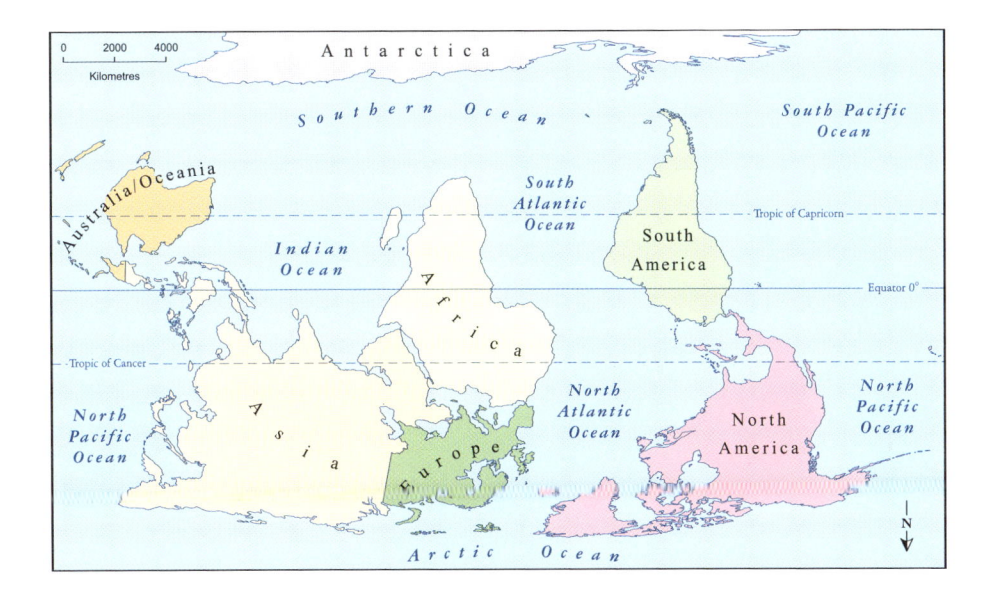

What is your first reaction when you look at this map? Where in the world might this be considered a normal way of picturing the world?

Why is it important to understand that people look at the world and at issues that face the world in different ways depending on their place in it? Discuss these ideas with a partner.

Key Ideas
In this chapter, you will learn about
- *your fundamental human rights*
- *human rights violations around the world*
- *Canada's role on the world stage*
- *ways you can contribute as a global citizen*

TAP into Active Citizenship

Being an active citizen sometimes involves thinking globally, but acting locally. You may have already discovered this as you have been planning, preparing, and executing your action plan. Now it's time to share your experiences with others.

As you work your way through this chapter, begin using all the materials in your Take Action Portfolio to prepare a final presentation on your project. Your presentation can take the form of a written report, an oral description, or a multimedia production using software such as PowerPoint. Whichever form you choose, be sure to include evidence of the specific actions you took and how successful your efforts were. What future plans do you have for making a difference?

Rights as Global Citizens

ACTIVATE YOUR THINKING

*The meaning of the word **citizen**, like the word democracy, has its origins in the Golden Age of Greece. Citizen was defined as a person who played a role in advancing Greek society. Today, a global citizen might be defined as anyone who works to make the world a better place.*

List the names of five people who you believe are making the world a better place. Consider people in your family or community, or people you have heard or read about. Beside each name, write one sentence to summarize what that person has done or is doing to improve the world.

citizen: a person who is a member of a particular country, and who has rights either because of being born there or because of having acquired citizenship to that country through immigration or through marriage

Canadian scholar Marshall McLuhan came up with the phrase "the global village." It describes the effect of communications technologies and mass media in bringing us into faster and more intimate contact with one another. This phrase was used before the Internet and satellite news made our knowledge of world events even more instantaneous.

Today, more than ever, global interdependence is a reality. It is important for us to know what is happening to people on the other side of the world because we are affected by their lives and the conditions in which they live.

Word building: many words are built from combining different word parts. The noun *interdependence* is built from the prefix *inter* (Latin for *between* or *among*), the verb *depend*, and the suffix *ence*.

The Universal Declaration of Human Rights

The United Nations (UN) was formed in 1945, at the end of World War II, in an effort to promote world peace and international security and co-operation. The idea was to create an organization where member nations could discuss and attempt to resolve world issues before conflicts escalated into war. Human rights also needed to be addressed, especially as the world was coming to terms with the horrifying reality of the Holocaust.

On December 10, 1948, the General Assembly of the United Nations adopted and proclaimed the Universal Declaration of Human Rights. The document states that all people have fundamental economic, cultural, social, political, and civil rights. The Assembly called on all UN Member countries to publicize the text of the Declaration, and to have the text and its message widely proclaimed and displayed in schools and other educational institutions. The Declaration contains, in addition to its preamble (introduction), 30 articles that outline people's universal rights. Some of the rights championed by the Declaration are

- the right to life, freedom, and personal safety
- the right to an education
- the right to participate fully in cultural life
- freedom from torture or cruel, inhumane treatment or punishment

- freedom of thought, religion, and conscience (personal sense of what is right and wrong)

The logo of the United Nations was approved in December 1946. It shows an image of the world surrounded by olive branches, which symbolize peace. The view of the world is an equidistant (equal distance apart) projection, centred on the North Pole. How does this view of the world accurately represent the goals of the UN?

The United Nations believed that as more people grew up knowing what was meant by human rights and why they were important, the world would become a better place. It was also important that all nations and people agreed to promote human rights and defend them. In this way, the nations of the world might help monitor, police, and deal with those countries that tried to limit such rights for their people. However, the Declaration is not legally binding. Individual countries decide to what extent they include these rights in their laws.

MILLENNIUM DEVELOPMENT GOALS

The Millennium Development Goals project is a UN-led initiative. These goals represent the world's main development challenges. Through a global partnership, these goals are to be achieved by 2015. What can you do to help make one of these goals a reality? What should Canada do?

1 = Eradicate Extreme Poverty and Hunger
2 = Achieve Universal Primary Education
3 = Promote Gender Equality and Empower Women
4 = Reduce Child Mortality
5 = Improve Maternal Health
6 = Combat HIV/AIDS, Malaria and Other Diseases
7 = Ensure Environmental Sustainability
8 = Global Partnership for Development

Global Citizenship 113

CITIZEN IN ACTION

Cardinal Paul-Émile Léger

Paul-Émile Léger was born in Montréal in 1904 and became a Roman Catholic priest at the age of 25. In 1967, after nearly 14 years as a Cardinal, he left his office to begin a new humanitarian mission in Africa, working among lepers and children with disabilities. With a passion to help the suffering, he spent 12 years in Africa, setting up clinics, hospitals, schools, and orphanages. He returned to Montréal in 1979 to work with a humanitarian organization that he had started. That same year he was awarded the Pearson Peace Medal, the first Canadian to receive this award for outstanding achievement in the field of international service and understanding.

What motivated Cardinal Léger to go to Africa? What humanitarian cause might motivate you to leave your home, friends, and family?

Cardinal Léger holds a child at the Centre for Handicapped Children, Yaoundé, Cameroon, in the early 1970s.

Over the years, the Declaration has inspired the creation of a number of international documents, such as the International Bill of Rights, the International Convention on the Elimination of All Forms of Racial Discrimination, and the International Convention on the Rights of the Child. It also makes the protection of human rights an important part of international law. Organizations such as Amnesty International, which observes and reports on cases of human rights violations around the world, refer to it as the basis of human rights. Finally, the *Universal Declaration of Human Rights* sets a standard of achievement for all nations to strive to achieve.

The *Canadian Charter of Rights and Freedoms* is partly inspired by the Universal Declaration of Human Rights, but there are differences between our Charter and the UN Declaration. The Canadian Charter is a legal instrument. All laws passed by Canadian governments are measured by what is written in the *Charter*. It also applies only to Canada. In addition, the *Charter* contains Canada-specific sections, such as the sections on minority language educational rights and the rights and freedoms of Aboriginal peoples in Canada.

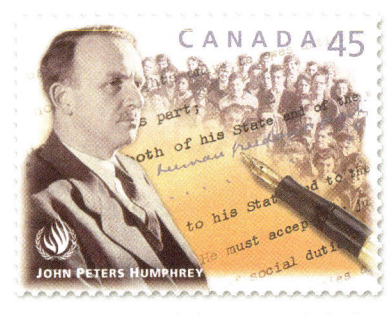

New Brunswick lawyer and diplomat John Peters Humphrey wrote the first draft of what eventually became the *Universal Declaration of Human Rights*. In 1998, to mark the 50th anniversary of the Declaration, Canada Post issued a stamp in Humphrey's honour. Humphrey also helped to establish Amnesty International Canada and the Canadian Human Rights Foundation.

CITIZEN IN ACTION

Ken Saro-Wiwa

Ken Saro-Wiwa was a Nigerian writer, poet, and environmentalist. He helped organize the Ogoni people, a small ethnic group in Nigeria, to fight against both the actions of a major international oil company (Shell Petroleum Development Company) and the dictatorship of Nigeria. He also helped establish the Movement for the Survival of the Ogoni People (MOSOP). In 1994, he was imprisoned on a made-up charge and executed along with eight other members of MOSOP.

December 10 is now recognized worldwide as Human Rights Day. Amnesty International Canada marks this day with an annual write-a-thon and fundraising event. Members, such as those pictured above, participate in writing letters of support and encouragement to prisoners who have been wrongfully detained. They also write persuasive letters to leaders who are in a position to right an injustice.

Protesters in Nigeria mark the 10th anniversary of the execution of their hero, Ken Saro-Wiwa.

School mission statements: school mission statements outline the principles that govern how the school is run, what goals it is trying to achieve, and what behaviours are expected from staff and students. Acronyms or other short forms can often be created from school mission statements (for example, W.I.S.H. might stand for Willingness, Integrity, Spirit, and Honour).

Before his execution, writers around the world tried to help free him, including those involved in PEN Canada. This organization, whose initials stand for **P**oets, **E**ssayists, and **N**ovelists, works to free imprisoned writers, to oppose censorship, and to create a network for writers living in exile in Canada. PEN's actions include organizing petitions, sending letters, faxes and postcards for the release of persecuted writers, and public awareness campaigns about freedom of expression. The inspiration for PEN's activities comes from Article 19 of the *Universal Declaration of Human Rights*, which guarantees freedom of opinion and the peaceable expression of such opinions, and section 2b of the *Canadian Charter of Rights and Freedoms*, which guarantees freedom of expression.

In a letter from prison, Ken Saro-Wiwa wrote:

"Whether I live or die is immaterial [unimportant]. It is enough to know that there are people who commit time, money and energy to fight this one evil among so many others... If they do not succeed today, they will succeed tomorrow. We must keep on striving to make the world a better place for all... each one contributing...in his or her own way."

Ken Saro-Wiwa's eldest son, Ken Wiwa, continued to champion his father's cause, becoming an influential human rights activist and writer. He established the Ken Saro-Wiwa Foundation, which is working toward setting up a secondary school in Ogoni and providing scholarships to Ogoni children. Ken Wiwa moved from Canada back to Nigeria at the invitation of the Nigerian government to help make change.

What beliefs and values are demonstrated by the actions of the Wiwas? How are they similar to or different from those of PEN Canada? Prepare a Venn diagram to show your ideas.

APPLY YOUR LEARNING

1. a) Why do you think it is important for human rights to be universal? Discuss your ideas with a partner.
   b) Work together to prepare a brief news report on the importance of the *Universal Declaration of Human Rights* either to you in particular, or to Canadians in general. Be prepared to present it orally to the class or a small group. Don't forget a headline to start your report!
2. a) Identify two similarities and two differences between the *Canadian Charter of Rights and Freedoms* and the *Universal Declaration of Human Rights*.
   b) If your school does not already have a mission statement, create one based on some of the principles outlined in both the

Global Citizenship

Universal Declaration of Human Rights and the *Canadian Charter of Rights and Freedoms*. If it does have one, identify how it reflects the principles in these two documents.

3. a) Research each of the rights identified in the *Universal Declaration of Human Rights.*

   b) Create a two-column chart in your notebook. In the first column, list each of the rights. In the second column, record examples of things you do every day that demonstrate how you have each of these rights.

Human Rights Violations Around the World

ACTIVATE YOUR THINKING

List five reasons why you would not want to live in a country under authoritarian rule.

Many countries around the world do not uphold the principles of the *Universal Declaration of Human Rights*. These are authoritarian countries and they are not always easy to identify. Words that would suggest a commitment to democratic principles and policies, such as *republic*, often appear in the names of these countries. A **republic** is a political system where the supreme power rests with the voting public who elect representatives to the government. However, such countries as the People's Republic of China, the Democratic People's Republic of Korea, the Islamic Republic of Iran, and the Republic of Zimbabwe are not democratic in the same way that Canada is democratic. One party led by a dictatorial president, who maintains power through intimidation and force, controls the political, economic, social, and religious aspects of each of these nations. The rights and freedoms of the people are severely limited.

republic: a political system where the supreme power rests with the voting public who elect representatives to the government. A republic is usually governed by these elected representatives and a president, but is not necessarily a democratic system of government.

The Islamic Republic of Iran

Throughout Iran's history, monarchs who have taken the title Shah have largely controlled the government. Despite the establishment of the nation's first parliament in 1906, the Shah was reinstated in 1953 after the prime minister was overthrown in a political plot supported by Britain and the United States.

The last Shah of Iran, Mohammad Reza Pahlavi, was very friendly to the United States and Britain, and he worked to westernize Iran and modernize its industries. He was also an autocrat (someone who rules with absolute power) who crushed or removed any interests or ideas opposed to his policies.

Among those who opposed the Shah was Ayatollah Khomeini, who in the early 1960s developed the idea of an Islamic government led by Islamic clerics (religious leaders). Khomeini was exiled (unwillingly banished from one's native country) by the Shah in 1964, but returned

116 *Passport to Civics*

Located on the Persian Gulf, Iran is the world's fourth largest oil-exporting country. This gives Iran a certain amount of economic influence in the world. This also means that many industrial nations in the west have an interest in the actions and policies of the Iranian government. What do you know about some of the countries that border Iran? Recall news reports you have heard in recent years.

in early 1979 after the effects of the Iranian Islamic Revolution forced the Shah into exile.

A new theocratic (faith-based ideology) constitution was drafted and accepted by popular vote in December 1979. The Ayatollah Khomeini became the Supreme Leader of Iran, a position held by Ali Khamenei in 2007. The Supreme Leader controls the armed forces and appoints many of the key positions in the judiciary, state radio and television networks, and six of the twelve members of the so-called 'Council of Guardians.'

After the Supreme Leader, the President is the next most powerful state official. Mahmoud Ahmadinejad was elected in June 2005, for a four-year term. His rise to power was of great concern to human rights defenders such as Human Rights Watch and activists in Iran, as he was backed by groups who opposed political and social reforms. Since then, Human Rights Watch has documented numerous human rights abuses against people who oppose his views. Iran's judiciary, in particular, has been at the centre of many serious human rights violations. These include arbitrary (random) arrest, detention without trial, torture to extract confessions, prolonged solitary confinement, and physical and psychological abuse.

Many of these human rights violations stem from the fact that there is no agency in place to investigate violations by agents of the government. There is no freedom of expression and opinion, so violations are not reported.

As you read the following case studies, identify the characteristics of authoritarian rule.

CASE STUDY 30: ZAHRA KAZEMI

In June, 2003, Iranian–Canadian photojournalist Zahra Kazemi died in the custody of Iran's public prosecutor and head of the intelligence unit. Autopsy reports revealed Kazemi died of severe blows to her head. The judiciary accused a low-ranking Intelligence Ministry official, Reza Ahmadi, of Kazemi's unintentional death. Ahmadi was then cleared of all charges in May 2004, after the judiciary proceeded with a hastily organized trial. Lawyers for Kazemi's family launched an appeal. At the appeal hearing in July 2005, lawyers demanded that the judiciary launch an investigation into charges of intentional homicide (murder). The judge refused the request. Iran's judicial system has done nothing further to try to identify or prosecute those responsible for Kazemi's murder.

CASE STUDY 31: REPUBLIC OF ZIMBABWE

The Republic of Zimbabwe in Africa was once a colony of Britain. In 1965 Southern Rhodesia, as the country was then called, declared unilateral (a one-sided decision) independence from Britain. At that time, the majority Black population was ruled by a government dominated by a minority White population. The minority also owned most of the land. In 1980, after a bitter civil war, Robert Mugabe, leader of the Zimbabwe African National Union (ZANU), which had been banned by the former government, became president.

Although people were at first optimistic, Mugabe and his party soon were accused of corruption and limiting the rights of the opposition. Amnesty International concluded that "as a result of persistent, long-term and systemic violations of human rights and the government's repeated and deliberate failure to bring to justice those who commit serious human rights violations, not all people in Zimbabwe could participate in the election process freely and without fear."

In December 2005, ZANU changed the constitution to cancel presidential elections in 2008 and extend President Robert Mugabe's term until 2010. Since acquiring a questionable two-thirds majority after the March

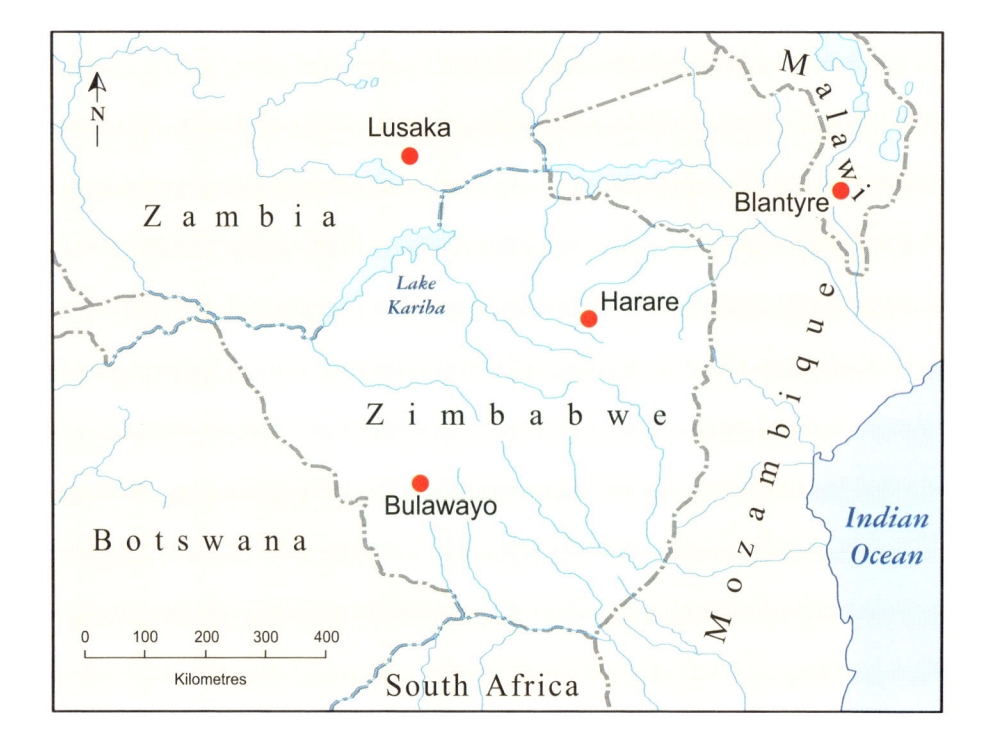

2005 elections, Mugabe has forced through a number of constitutional amendments intended to suppress any challenges to his power.

APPLY YOUR LEARNING

1. List two similarities and two differences between Iran's government system and that of other authoritarian countries.
2. What might happen if the world ignores the human rights violations that occur in places such as Zimbabwe? Identify three ways the people who live there as well as the rest of the world might be affected. Discuss your ideas with a partner.

Rwanda

ACTIVATE YOUR THINKING

Recall the impact European arrival in North America had on Aboriginal peoples. Write down three consequences of this contact. Compare your ideas with a partner. How might some of these consequences have been avoided?

In the late 1800s, European nations raced to colonize Africa in an effort to control its many natural resources, such as gold, copper, and salt. In their haste and greed, these countries divided up the continent without regard for the pre-existing cultural and language differences among the African population. The legacy of this haphazard division has been political instability and racial discord. The civil war that erupted in Rwanda is a case in point.

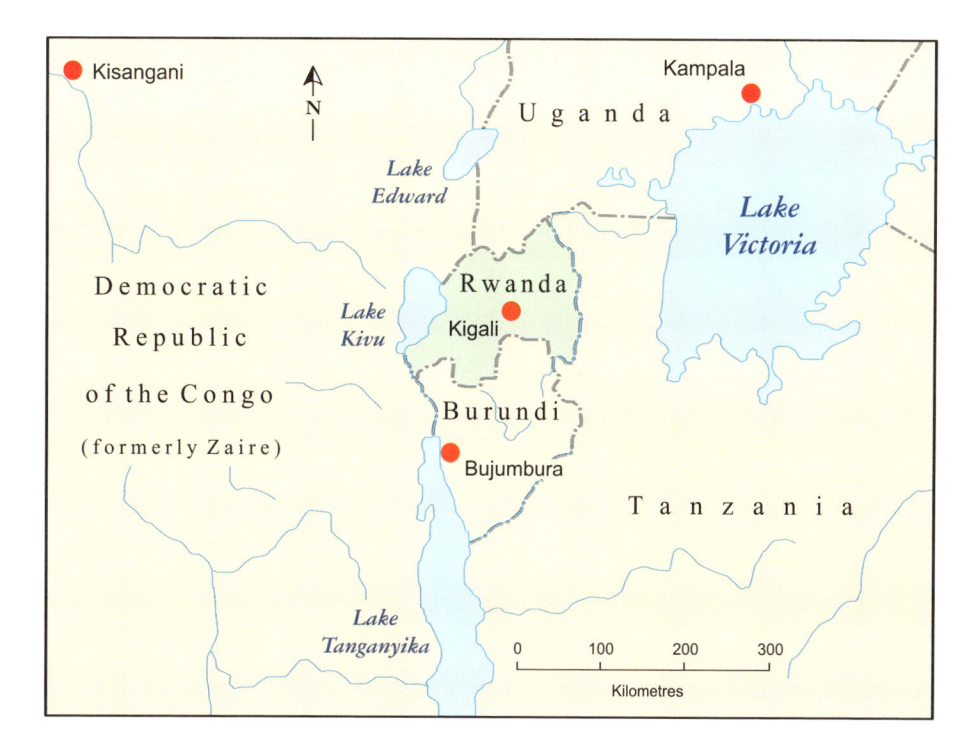

Global Citizenship 119

Background to the Rwandan Crisis

Prior to colonization, the population of Rwanda consisted of two ethnic groups—the Hutus and the Tutsis—who co-existed as equals. Under Belgian rule, however, the minority Tutsi population had enjoyed more power than the majority Hutu population. When Rwanda became independent in 1962, the Hutu majority took power and the roles were reversed. As a result ethnic tensions escalated in the country, with increasing violence between the two groups.

In 1993, the UN sent a peacekeeping force of 2500 soldiers to try to hold a ceasefire between the Hutus and the Tutsis. Most of these soldiers came from Belgium or Bangladesh, but it was Major General Romeo Dallaire of Canada who actually led the peacekeeping mission.

In January, 1994, General Dallaire sent a message to UN headquarters in New York. He requested protection for an informant who had told him of a secret stockpile of weapons, of Hutu plans to exterminate (kill) the Tutsis, and of intentions to provoke and kill Belgian peacekeeping troops so Belgium would withdraw from Rwanda. General Dallaire also pleaded for reinforcements, as his peacekeeping force had been reduced to 270 soldiers. (The population of Rwanda in 1994 totalled 7 million.) General Dallaire's request was ignored by the UN. Three months later everything the informant had said came true.

Rwandan Genocide

Genocide is the systematic destruction of a nation or an ethnic or religious group. It implies a co-ordinated plan, aimed at total extermination of individuals who are considered members of the targeted group. In 1948, after World War II and the Holocaust in Europe, the UN passed a resolution called the Convention on the Prevention and Punishment of the Crime of Genocide. Article 2 of the resolution agreed that genocide can mean any of the following acts committed with the intent of destroying, in whole or in part, any national, ethnic, racial, or religious group, such as

(a) killing members of the group;
(b) causing serious bodily or mental harm to members of the group;
(c) deliberately inflicting on the group conditions of life meant to bring about its physical destruction in whole or in part;
(d) imposing measures intended to prevent births within the group;
(e) forcibly transferring children of the group to another group.

When a plane carrying Rwandan President Habyarimana, a Hutu, was shot down on April 6, 1994, the Hutu extremists, who believed the President was going to agree to peace accords ending the hostilities between the two ethnic groups, started killing Tutsis. In order to dehumanize the Tutsis and whip up Hutu feelings against them, a radio station referred to Tutsis as "cockroaches." This hate campaign was all too successful, and thousands were murdered on the first day. Some United Nations' troops tried to protect civilians, but the UN

genocide: the systematic destruction of a nation, or an ethnic or religious group

Cemetery in Nyanza-Rebero, Rwanda, marking graves of genocide victims.

prohibited them from intervening. The next day, ten Belgian soldiers with the UN were tricked by Hutus into giving up their weapons and, having done so, were then tortured and murdered.

On April 9 France and Belgium sent troops to rescue their citizens, as did the Americans. The Red Cross estimated that, by April 11, thousands of Rwandan Tutsis had already been murdered. On April 21, the UN Security Council voted unanimously to withdraw most of its forces. By mid-May the International Red Cross estimated that half a million Rwandans had been killed. When faced with international TV news reports depicting genocide, the UN Security Council voted to send up to 5000 soldiers to Rwanda. However, the Security Council did not include a timetable, and so never sent the troops in time to stop the massacre. By mid-July the Tutsi forces had captured Kigali, the capital. The Hutu government fled to Zaire. It is estimated that 800 000 Rwandans were killed by fellow Rwandans in 100 days.

What does this photo suggest the people of Rwanda hope for?

The Aftermath

In November 1994, the UN established the International Criminal Tribunal to prosecute Rwandan officials for genocide, using the 1948 Genocide Convention. The first judgment was on September 2, 1998, when Paul Akayesu, former mayor of Taba, a small town in central Rwanda, was found guilty of nine counts of genocide and of crimes against humanity. He was sentenced to three life terms plus 80 years. He is appealing his sentence.

Another tragic consequence of the Rwandan genocide was that hundreds of thousands of children were either orphaned or separated from their parents. Most ended up in orphanages or children's centres. Living conditions were poor, with overcrowding and a lack of such basics as clothing and education.

It is estimated that up to 10 percent of Rwanda's children are orphaned today. Some were adopted without the permission of surviving family members. Others were sent to live with foster families, who often mistreated them. Still others formed child-led households; all are unprotected. Because rape was a common weapon, many Rwandans contracted HIV/AIDS, and this has added to the number of children without families. The number of children killed in Rwanda in 1994 was 300 000—the same number of children born in Canada in 2003.

In Kigali, on May 7, 1998, then UN Secretary-General Kofi Annan apologized to the parliament of Rwanda.

> "...The world must deeply repent [regret] this failure. Rwanda's tragedy was the world's tragedy. All of us who cared about Rwanda, all of us who witnessed its suffering, fervently [strongly] wish that we could have prevented the genocide. Looking back now, we see the signs which then were not recognized. Now we know that what we did was not nearly enough—not enough to save Rwanda from itself, not enough to honour the ideals for which the United Nations exists. We will not deny that, in their greatest hour of need, the world failed the people of Rwanda...."

Do you agree with the UN Secretary-General's description of the events in Rwanda as an act of genocide? Explain your thinking.

CITIZEN IN ACTION

Stephen Lewis

Stephen Lewis is a passionate and determined humanitarian who has actively worked to improve the human condition, both at home and abroad. His first arena of active citizenship was as leader of the Ontario New Democratic Party for eight years, during which time he became leader of the Official Opposition. He also served as Canadian Ambassador to the United Nations, and as the Deputy Executive Director of UNICEF in New York.

In 2004, Stephen Lewis was presented with the Pearson Peace Medal by the United Nations Association in Canada

35 Stephen Lewis served as the UN Secretary-General's Special Envoy for HIV/AIDS in Africa and a Commissioner for the World Health Organization's (WHO) Commission on the Social Determinants of Health. His mission with WHO was to bring the issue of AIDS to world attention. This he successfully did, his work culminating in the World AIDS Conference held in Toronto in August 2006. He is also a director of the Stephen Lewis Foundation, an organization dedicated to easing the pain of HIV/AIDS in Africa. His term as Special Envoy ended in December 2006.

How might Stephen Lewis's political background and experiences have helped him in his efforts to promote the plight of Africans around the world?

36 On a more positive note Rwanda's new constitution, passed in 2003, ensured that the electoral system of proportional representation would guarantee some seats to women. It also provided for gender equality. By 2007 women had taken a significant leadership role in rebuilding Rwanda. Rwanda has the most women in parliament in the world at close to 50 percent (Canada has 21 percent). "It's the first time we have Hutus and Tutsis (women) sitting together and talking about poverty. Women talking about development."

APPLY YOUR LEARNING

1. a) Create a timeline of key events in the Rwandan crisis. Limit your timeline to ten entries.
   b) Choose three of the events on your timeline and write a response to the actions of all those involved.
2. Debate this resolution: "The United Nations should always intervene when there is a potential genocide." Participate in small groups (two versus two). Be sure each person gets a chance to explain her or his arguments.
3. Who do you think bears the greatest responsibility for the situation that developed in Rwanda? Consider European colonists, Hutus, Tutsis, the UN Security Council, and UN peacekeepers. Explain your reasoning in a supported opinion paragraph.

Child Soldiers

ACTIVATE YOUR THINKING

Have you ever felt pressured to do something you didn't want to do? How did you handle it? Record your experiences in your notebook.

37 The International Convention on the Rights of the Child, passed by the United Nations in 1989, recognized that children's rights are human

The Coalition to Stop the Use of Child Soldiers works to raise awareness of the plight of child soldiers.

rights, not special rights or even optional rights. It called for all children to have access to education and health care, and identified the need to protect children under the age of 18 from all forms of discrimination. It covered such issues as child labour and child abuse; however, the problem of child soldiers was not included.

The international challenge of children being forced into becoming soldiers is one of great concern for many organizations. There are three main reasons why children are used in conflict:

- With technological advances, weapons are smaller, lighter, and cheaper.
- Children are easily influenced and can be numbed to violence.
- The army often promises money to poor families for the services of their children. At other times, the children are simply kidnapped and kept under control with threats of violence toward them and their families.

According to the Canadian International Development Agency (CIDA), there are over 300 000 children under 18 (some as young as 7) fighting in armed conflicts around the world.

As you read the words of former child soldiers in the case study that follows, reflect on the circumstances that led to their becoming involved in armed conflict.

CASE STUDY 32: CHILDREN IN COMBAT

"I ran away (to join an armed group) to escape a marriage I didn't like."
— teenage girl soldier in Sri Lanka

"Russia has turned us into cattle. It is driving our youth into the arms of whoever comes along first and says, 'Go with us.'"
— mother in Chechnya

"When they came to my village, they asked my older brother whether he was ready to join the militia. He was just 17 and he said no; they shot him in the head. Then they asked me if I was ready to sign, so what could I do—I didn't want to die."
— former child soldier taken when he was 13, Democratic Republic of Congo (BBC report)

"They give you a gun and you have to kill the best friend you have. They do it to see if they can trust you. If you don't kill him, your friend will be ordered to kill you. I had to do it because otherwise I would have been killed. That's why I got out. I couldn't stand it any longer."
— 17-year-old Colombian boy who joined a paramilitary group at the age of 7, when he was a street child

"I did learn some things when I was with the rebels. I learnt how to shoot, how to lay anti-personnel mines and how to live on the run. I especially knew how to use an AK-47 twelve-inch, which I could dismantle in less than one minute. When I turned 12 they gave me an RPG [rocket propelled grenade], because I had proved myself in battle."
— kidnapped 19-year-old soldier, Palaro District, northern Uganda

Children who are recruited as soldiers are denied both an education and protection, and are often unable to access health care. Once out of the conflict, they face difficult challenges getting back into society. Girls are especially difficult to help, because boys are given priority when it comes to accessing available services. Some girls, raped while they were soldiers, return with babies, and may even be rejected by their families and communities.

Solutions

Graça Machel was appointed in 1994 by the Secretary-General of the United Nations as an independent expert to lead a study on the Impact of Armed Conflict on Children. She was chosen for her reputation as an educator and advocate for children. One conference was held in Winnipeg, Manitoba, in September 2000. This conference was groundbreaking because it included youth from Canada and around the world and became a model for future discussions. They made recommendations to the international community and expressed strong opinions on how to improve the lives of children. The conference prepared and presented the final agenda for the UN Special Session on Children in 2002.

In their closing statement to the conference, the youth included this call to action:

> *"Let's make it possible for the voices of children to be heard in the global community. This organization could do this through activities such as lobbying, pressuring governments, and running campaigns to adopt better policies concerning children and war. In addition to these tactics, we would also like to use resources that are currently available to create a worldwide network of youth, which will be focused on this issue, and determined to make life better for those who are suffering. Holding discussions and workshops to educate children regarding their rights, advising and facilitating [assisting] program development, and identifying priorities [most important steps] for research, are some examples of what the youth can do if the opportunity would be given."*

In 2000, after much negotiation, the governments of most countries agreed on a new international treaty to ban the use of children as soldiers. The new Optional Protocol to the Convention on the Rights of the Child agreed that the minimum age for participating in any military conflict would be 18. Also, the minimum age for compulsory recruitment would be 18. This new protocol (set of rules) changed the definition of *age of a child* from 15 to 18. It finally passed by a vote in the UN in 2002.

Under the terms of the protocol,
- governments must take all possible measures to ensure that no one under 18 participates directly in conflict

Graça Machel, United Nations chair of the Impact of Armed Conflict on Children study, and wife of Nelson Mandela

This image appears on a website that connects to the report on War-Affected Children. Why would this image be selected? What impact does it have on you, the viewer?

Adolescent boys wearing civilian clothes walk away from the weapons they once carried as child soldiers in Sudan. What feelings do you get when you look at the picture and why?

- governments cannot conscript (force to enrol) into the military anyone under 18
- governments must pass laws to make it illegal for any armed group to recruit anyone under 18 into their organization, and must also take other measures to prevent the use of children by these groups
- governments must disarm any children who were recruited in violation of the protocol, help them heal, and bring them back into society
- governments must submit a progress report within two years of agreeing to the protocol, and every five years after that

CITIZEN IN ACTION

Craig Kielburger

The problem of child soldiers is not the only human rights violation requiring international pressure. Child labour is another major concern. Craig Kielburger was only 12 years old when he discovered in a newspaper article that there were over 250 million child labourers in the world, often working in dangerous conditions. Along with a few friends, he founded Free the Children, a network of children helping children around the world through education. It now involves over 1 million young people in more than 45 countries. "The mission is to free young people from the idea that they are powerless to bring about positive social change, and to act to improve the lives of young people everywhere."

In addition to Free the Children, Kielburger started a youth leadership organization in 1999 with his brother Marc called Leaders Today, which delivers training experiences to more than 350 000 youth around the world every year. Programs such as Volunteer Ambassadors is a hands-on training program developed for high schools interested in providing Grade 10 students with the tools necessary to become active local and global citizens.

Complete this sentence in your notebook: I believe that education is the key to bringing about positive social change because....

Craig Kielburger, founder of Free the Children and Leaders Today

APPLY YOUR LEARNING

1. a) As you read the statement from youth on page 125, what do you think should be the first priority of the United Nations in response to this call to action?
   b) If you had attended the conference, what would you like to have said? Prepare a short speech and deliver it to a small group.
2. With the assistance of your teacher, research one other issue that relates to the plight of children around the world (for example, the impact of natural disasters, hunger and malnutrition, violence and the gang culture, birth registration, and sexual exploitation). Include a key article and a summary of your research in your Take Action Portfolio.

Persuasive language: a persuasive speech uses strong and specific words to convey a message, as well as statements that include the listeners. For example:
- I believe that… and I am sure that you do, too.
- It is clear to all of us that….
- We all experience… and that means that….

Canada on the World Stage

ACTIVATE YOUR THINKING

What are you most proud of about being a Canadian? What are you least proud of? If you could be a citizen of any other country in the world, which would you choose? Why?

Canada has earned a reputation around the world as a champion of human rights, a nation of peacekeepers, and a leader in providing aid and relief to those devastated by poverty or natural disaster. We have assumed this role on the world stage not out of a sense of generosity, but out of a sense of responsibility as a global citizen.

Canada's Role in International Affairs

The interconnectedness of the global village makes it difficult sometimes to decide what to do when problems erupt. Think about your circle of friends. What happens when two of the people in the group have a disagreement? Do you remain neutral, or do you side with one person against the other? What if the rest of the group decides on a course of action to resolve the conflict that you don't support? What impact do conflicts such as these have on the group's relationship over time?

One way countries express their dissatisfaction with the policies or conduct of another nation is through diplomatic means. A representative from one country meets or speaks with representatives from the offending country to explain the problem in an attempt to negotiate change. Often, these meetings become a "war of words," with two or more nations exchanging insults, accusations, and threats.

In December 2005, North Korea, an authoritarian nation, accused the United States of human rights violations. It cited US conduct in the war in Iraq and its treatment of Iraqi prisoners. In response Alexander Vershbow, US ambassador to South Korea, referred to North

Korea as "a criminal regime," adding that "North Korea's people remain oppressed by a regime whose policies have failed to address even the most basic needs of its citizens. The people of North Korea are unable to enjoy even the simplest freedoms that we in the free world often take for granted."

Another way countries try to pressure other nations into changing their behaviour is by boycotting (refusing to buy or sell) certain goods from the nation in question, restricting trade, and ceasing the supply of aid. Yet another way is through military action, especially when the peace of a region is threatened or lives are being lost.

Despite the existence of the Universal Declaration of Human Rights, not all nations agree with or uphold the ideals that it contains. You have read about several nations in which the leaders have taken actions that are actually harmful to their own citizens. In 1993, the General Assembly of the United Nations recommended the establishment of a position of High Commissioner for Human Rights responsible for United Nations human rights activities. The High Commissioner's role would be to promote and protect all human rights—civil, political, economic, social, and cultural. As you might imagine, this is a very big job! Some of the issues the Commissioner is currently working on include children's rights; being jailed without cause; the disappearances of people for speaking out against their leaders; freedom of religion and belief; and bioethics (the moral and ethical dilemmas posed by medical research and the use of advanced technology).

In 2004, Canadian lawyer and Supreme Court Justice Louise Arbour was appointed to the position of UN High Commissioner for Human Rights. Prior to this appointment, Louise Arbour had served as chief prosecutor of war crimes and human rights abuses before the International Tribunal for Rwanda and the former Yugoslavia.

UN High Commissioner for Human Rights Louise Arbour speaks to members of a local community in civil war-ravaged Sudan in May 2006.

CITIZEN IN ACTION

Jody Williams

Among the many concerns of the UN High Commissioner for Human Rights are the indiscriminate and devastating effects of anti-personnel landmines. A landmine is an explosive weapon that is placed on or just under the ground, exploding when stepped on, tripped over, or picked up. The result is death or severe injury, and the impact on mine-affected communities has reached crisis proportions.

Jody Williams is a co-founder of, and works as a co-ordinator for, the International Campaign to Ban Landmines (ICBL). She, along with the ICBL, was awarded the Nobel Peace Prize in 1997 for the ICBL's role in trying to ban the use of anti-personnel landmines. The problem, Williams says, is that "Once peace is declared the landmine does not recognize that peace. The landmine is eternally prepared to take victims. It is the perfect soldier."

Recent statistics estimate there are between 45 and 50 million landmines buried in at least 70 countries around the world, and not all countries have signed on to the treaty to ban them. Clearly, there is still a great deal of work to be done. But as Jody Williams points out, "Ordinary people, when they believe in themselves and what they want to do, can achieve extraordinary things. What makes a person extraordinary? It's what they do, not how they're born."

Identify three examples from your own life, news reports, or this book that support Jody Williams' claim that ordinary people can achieve extraordinary things.

The Ottawa Treaty or Mine Ban Treaty was spearheaded by Canada in 1997 and has since become part of international humanitarian law. Here, students create a shoe pile in a Winnipeg mall to symbolize the destructiveness of land mines, since survivors of land mines' blasts have often had their feet and legs blown off.

As the 20th century ended, the international community, including Canada, agreed to adopt a treaty to create the world's first independent and permanent International Criminal Court (ICC). Before the establishment of this court, there had been no way of holding to account those who committed the gravest of crimes, namely genocide, war crimes, and crimes against humanity. The ICC considers itself a court of last resort. It will step in only if cases are not investigated by a nation's existing justice system or if the proceedings are in any way corrupt.

Canadian lawyer and diplomat Philippe Kirsch was chosen to lead a group, the so-called Committee of the Whole, at the Rome Conference, held from July 15 to 17, 1998, in Rome, Italy. This committee was the primary negotiator at the Conference, and Canada's leadership role was a major factor in balancing the differing points of view of other countries. Canada was also instrumental in achieving an eventual agreement in such areas as the jurisdiction (area of legal authority) of the International Criminal Court and the definition of war crimes.

The Rome Statute of the International Criminal Court was adopted when 120 countries agreed in principle to the treaty conditions. Only seven countries, including China, Israel, Iraq, and the United States, refused to agree. Why? For various reasons these countries are not comfortable being judged by the international community. In June 2000, Canada was the first country to pass significant laws to implement the International Criminal Court.

The treaty began its official existence in April 2002, when ten countries deposited with the UN their ratifications (approval) of the conditions. As of October 2007, the ICC had 105 member countries.

The Preparatory Committee set up to work out such details as the legal process for trying cases was again led by Philippe Kirsch.

Canadian lawyer and diplomat Philippe Kirsch was elected as a judge and the president of the International Criminal Court in February 2003.

Global Citizenship

APPLY YOUR LEARNING

1. a) Brainstorm with a partner the qualities you think a judge who sits on the International Criminal Court should have.
   b) Does it make a difference what type of law background or experience the judge has? Discuss this question with another pair group.
2. a) Why do you suppose Canada is so involved in international human rights initiatives?
   b) What reasons might there be for some countries not to be involved?

Canada's Response to Natural Disasters

ACTIVATE YOUR THINKING

List all the ways you have contributed to the solutions to world problems in the last few years; for example, by contributing to tsunami relief. Create a second list describing actions other people have taken to help.

As 2005 began, the news was dominated by reports of the destruction that was caused by tsunamis (destructive ocean waves) that hit coastal regions of Southeast Asia on December 26, 2004. As the year progressed, other disasters caused by nature would unfold. The Caribbean and the southeastern United States would live through a record-setting hurricane season that would see much of New Orleans, Louisiana, flooded and destroyed. Strong earthquakes would cause terrible devastation as winter approached in Pakistan. The world's citizens would be called on as never before to respond to these catastrophic events.

Tsunami in Southeast Asia

The world response to the devastation caused by the tsunami was immediate and continues today. The Red Cross, along with other relief and government agencies around the world, sprang into action.

In the case of Canada, a reconnaissance team (military staff sent ahead of other teams to check out the situation) assessed what was required to assist the region. They set out from Ottawa for Colombo, Sri Lanka, on December 30. On January 2, 2005, then Prime Minister Paul Martin announced that Canada would be sending the Canadian Armed Forces Disaster Assistance Response Team (DART) to Ampara, a district of Sri Lanka of approximately 600 000 people. This was one of the districts most affected by the tsunamis, with an estimated 10 400 people killed. Approximately 180 000 people were displaced, and damage to hospitals, roads, and water supplies was significant.

The creation of DART increased the federal government's ability to respond to requests for aid either in Canada or anywhere else in the

Medical technicians with the Canadian Forces Disaster Assistance Response Team (DART) look at the rash on a young girl's arm while inspecting tsunami damage in the Ampara district, January 12, 2005.

world. Canada continues to be an important provider of international humanitarian assistance and emergency relief.

At the one-year anniversary of the tsunami, governments and organizations continued to help rebuild the devastated areas. In December 2005, the Ontario government announced that it would contribute $400 000 toward the cost of two new schools, one in Sri Lanka and the other in Indonesia.

The Ontario Citizenship and Immigration Minister, Mike Colle, summed up the continued response by saying, "As the one-year anniversary of the tsunami approaches, it reminds us that Ontarians are citizens of the world. Our people come from some 200 countries, so when something happens, we respond."

CITIZENS IN ACTION

International Federation of Red Cross and Red Crescent Societies

The International Federation of Red Cross and Red Crescent Societies was founded in 1919 in Paris after World War I. Red Cross leaders realized that co-operation helped develop expertise, and that the individual societies could achieve more if they worked together. Five founding member societies had originally formed the federation, but now there are over 181 members.

The Federation's first mission was to help typhus and famine victims in Poland in 1920, a civilian rather than a military emergency and the only one undertaken in that year. Today, the Federation operates over 80 relief operations per year. Its seven core principles are humanity, impartiality, neutrality, independence, voluntary service, unity, and universality.

Red Cross Activities, 1919–2006	
Floods, cyclones, storms	569
Socio-economic problems (e.g., literacy)	438
Population movements (e.g., refugees displaced by conflict or natural disaster)	336
Food security, droughts	218
Earthquakes, volcanoes	181
Mixed regional programs (e.g., safe drinking water)	216
Health and care (e.g., epidemic control, health promotion)	136
General assistance	122
Total missions	2216

The Red Cross/Red Crescent Societies work together to respond to disasters by providing relief and preventative health-care services. Diseases cause more deaths than natural disasters or armed conflicts together. The combined effects of HIV/AIDS, tuberculosis, malaria, and water and sanitation-related diseases together kill 13 million people every year. While the media focus on natural disasters, the Red Cross/Red Crescent societies work to improve the lives of citizens around the world by providing healthier environments.

List three reasons why organizations might join together to make a difference.

CITIZEN IN ACTION

Frank Stronach

Frank Stronach arrived in Ontario in 1954, virtually penniless, as an immigrant from Austria. He started a small tool-and-die business, which he then built into Magna International, a multi-billion dollar global supplier of auto parts.

Within a week of the Hurricane Katrina disaster in August 2005, which devastated the Gulf coast of the southern United States, Frank Stronach flew several hundred people to Magna's new horse-training facilities in Boynton Beach, Florida. There evacuees were housed in facilities intended for grooms and thoroughbred trainers, fed at a brand new state-of-the-art cafeteria, and provided with medical care and new clothes courtesy of local residents. Frank Stronach pledged to build a 325-hectare organic farm and small village in Louisiana where people could live, find jobs, and start over. "We want to show the world that no matter where you're born, no matter how poor you are, that you can succeed in life."

In addition to the damage caused by Katrina's 230 km/h winds and rain, two levees that held back waters from the Gulf of Mexico broke. Eighty percent of the city of New Orleans was covered in water, which rose in some areas to a depth of six metres.

Magnaville gives Hurricane Katrina survivors a fresh start.

True to his word, and with the help of numerous organizations and volunteers, the first phase of Magnaville opened in December 2005 with about 100 residents. Residents can live rent free for up to five years in the furnished, air-conditioned, and landscaped mobile homes while they look for work in nearby towns or on the onsite farm.

On a scale of 1 to 5, with 5 being outstanding, rate Frank Stronach's contribution to Hurricane Katrina relief efforts. Explain your rating.

Earthquake in Pakistan

Over 80 000 people died in the 7.6-magnitude earthquake that rocked northern Pakistan, Kashmir, and parts of India on October 8, 2005. Because the quake happened on a school day, 17 000 school children died when their classrooms collapsed around them. An additional 72 000 people were injured.

Within days of the earthquake, the government of Canada announced that DART would be sent to Pakistan to help in relief efforts. The government allotted approximately $20 million to earthquake relief, which included matching donations that individual Canadians made to agencies targeting Pakistan earthquake relief.

Also involved in relief efforts was the United Nations High Commissioner for Refugees (UNHCR). This agency is responsible for helping refugees (people seeking safety and protection in another place) who, for political or natural causes, have been forced from their homes.

As you read the following case study, identify what challenges the UNHCR faced and what measures they took in response to the earthquake in Pakistan.

The epicentre is where the earthquake reaches the Earth's surface. It was close to heavily populated areas in Pakistan.

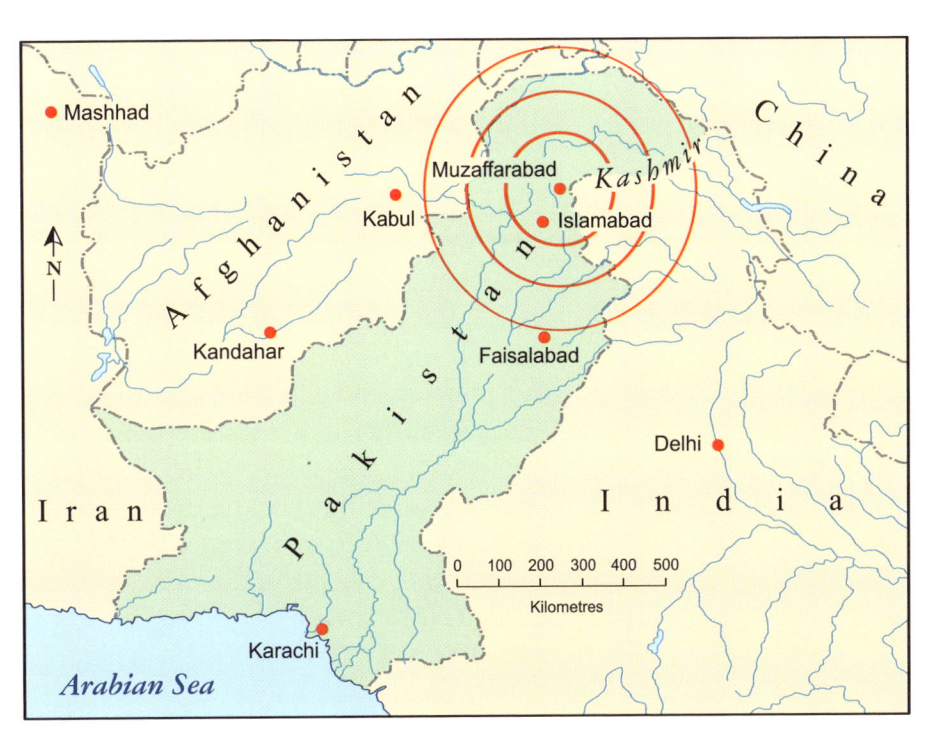

Global Citizenship 133

CASE STUDY 33: RESPONSE TO PAKISTAN EARTHQUAKE

UNHCR Boosts Relief to Pakistan Earthquake Victims

By Lisa Schlein

Geneva
23 December 2005

Refugee camp in Muzaffarabad, Pakistan, December 2005

The United Nations refugee agency says it is boosting its distribution of winterized materials to earthquake victims in Pakistan. UNHCR says thousands of survivors still are unprepared to weather the sub-freezing temperatures gripping the Himalayan mountain villages....

UNHCR Spokesman Ron Redmond says the agency is boosting its winterization campaign with a new round of aid distribution in camps for quake survivors. These include hundreds of thousands of blankets and plastic sheets. He says stoves and other supplies also are being distributed.

"But, with the cold weather, people are inevitably going to try to stay warm with candles and stoves inside their tents," explained Mr. Redmond. "That is going to increase the risk of fires. We are working with the authorities to try to find safe ways to provide heating in the camps, including mud fireplaces, which are made by Afghan refugees. We have actually enlisted Afghan refugees in this effort, because they are quite experienced in making it through the winter in very rudimentary shelter...."

Another concern is spontaneous camps. UNHCR Spokesman Ron Redmond said nearly 127 000 people are living in 335 squalid camps. "Our mobile teams are working in those camps to try to fix latrines, bathrooms, communal kitchens," he explained. "So far, they have managed to improve facilities in 50 of the camps. We also are working with UNICEF, OXFAM and other partners to provide water. We are decongesting some of the more overcrowded spontaneous camps, helping people to move elsewhere."...

WHAT CAN YOU DO?

Join an NGO

Non-governmental organizations (NGOs) are non-profit, voluntary citizens' groups organized at the local, national, or international level. Unconnected with any government, they operate independently, focusing on issues they believe are important, such as those related to human rights, health, or the environment. NGOs serve as watchdogs, bringing citizens' concerns to government attention, monitoring policies, and checking that international agreements are followed. They are invaluable participants in humanitarian efforts around the world. 78

In the aftermath of the earthquake in Pakistan, numerous NGOs provided relief to victims—by distributing food, tents for shelter, warm blankets, medicine, and safe drinking water. 79

OXFAM Canada is one NGO dedicated to fighting poverty and injustice around the world. It is part of an international organization that originated in England at Oxford University during World War II. 80

134 *Passport to Civics*

Members of Direct Relief International assist earthquake survivors in northern Pakistan.

Organizations such as OXFAM provide opportunities for people to actively support their goals by donating, volunteering, becoming a member, or working with them as a career. In the six months after the earthquake in Pakistan, OXFAM provided water and sanitation facilities for approximately 580 000 men, women, and children. It distributed winterized tents and temporary shelter kits to 370 000 people, and helped nearly 60 000 people rebuild their livelihoods.

Direct Relief International, established in 1948, has furnished $6 million in emergency medical aid in response to the same earthquake. Direct Relief International is not affiliated (linked) with any religious, political, or government organization.

Research other NGOs that participated in relief efforts in Pakistan. How many of them are Canadian?

APPLY YOUR LEARNING

1. What criteria do you think should be used to decide what help Canada will provide when a disaster occurs? Create a list of five criteria, and then compare your list with others in a small group. Try to agree as a group on a final list of five and present your criteria to the class.
2. Find an article on a recent or ongoing natural disaster that describes what people around the world are doing to provide aid. Highlight key sentences in the article that identify these actions. Place the article in your Take Action Portfolio under a title of your choice.

Working Together for Change

ACTIVATE YOUR THINKING

What are the advantages of working with other people to solve a problem or change a situation? What are the disadvantages?

The idea that individuals can and should take action on issues of local, national, and global significance is the cornerstone, or most important building block, of democracy. Individuals have talked of this for centuries. As you read the following quotations, think about what they all have in common.

> *It is better to light one candle than to curse the darkness.*
> — *Chinese proverb*

> *You must be the change you wish to see in the world.*
> — *Mahatma Gandhi (1869–1948), Hindu nationalist and spiritual leader*

No one could make a greater mistake than he who did nothing because he could do only a little.
— Edmund Burke (1729–1797), British statesman and philosopher

CITIZENS IN ACTION

Doctors Without Borders (Médecins Sans Frontières)
Engineers Without Borders

Médecins Sans Frontières (MSF) was established in 1971 by a small group of French doctors who had worked in Africa. When they returned to France, they wanted to find a way to respond quickly and effectively to public health emergencies, without political, economic, or religious influences. They have provided medical help to people caught in military conflicts, natural disasters, epidemics, and famines. They were awarded the Nobel Peace Prize for their efforts. The Canadian branch was founded in 1991 with the aim of recruiting and training staff, raising awareness of international projects, and working with government agencies. MSF members have worked in many war-torn areas, such as the Republic of Congo, Colombia, Haiti, Iraq, and Afghanistan, risking and sometimes losing their lives to help others.

Engineers Without Borders is a Canadian organization founded in 2000 by George Roter and Parker Mitchell. This charitable organization works to increase awareness of, and concern for, the situation of people in under-developed communities, while at the same time trying to increase the developed world's awareness and knowledge of world poverty. Engineers Without Borders encourages change at a local level by showing the different ways people can take action to improve their well being.

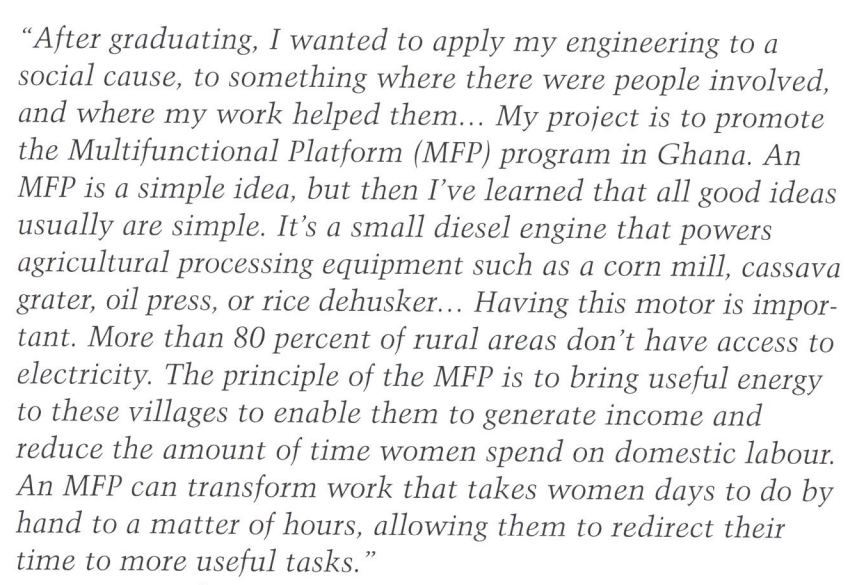

Mike Quinn (right) is currently working on an Engineers Without Borders project in Zambia.

"After graduating, I wanted to apply my engineering to a social cause, to something where there were people involved, and where my work helped them... My project is to promote the Multifunctional Platform (MFP) program in Ghana. An MFP is a simple idea, but then I've learned that all good ideas usually are simple. It's a small diesel engine that powers agricultural processing equipment such as a corn mill, cassava grater, oil press, or rice dehusker... Having this motor is important. More than 80 percent of rural areas don't have access to electricity. The principle of the MFP is to bring useful energy to these villages to enable them to generate income and reduce the amount of time women spend on domestic labour. An MFP can transform work that takes women days to do by hand to a matter of hours, allowing them to redirect their time to more useful tasks."
— Mike Quinn, working on a 2003 Engineers Without Borders project in Ghana, West Africa

What do Engineers Without Borders and Doctors Without Borders have in common? Prepare a Venn diagram to show both the similarities and differences between them.

Approaches to Active Citizenship

Individuals can sometimes have the greatest impact when they work with others. There are opportunities to combine skills, expand connections, and reach more people. As well-known anthropologist Margaret Mead once stated, "Never doubt that a small group of committed citizens can change the world. Indeed, it is the only thing that ever has."

The challenge for you as a global citizen is to determine how, and through what agency, you can best be active in helping the causes in which you believe. Here are some suggestions:

- Choose a problem or issue that you feel passionate about. Volunteering is a great way to get exposure to a variety of issues, and gives you a very good feeling of accomplishment. It can be as basic as picking up garbage in your neighbourhood or cleaning up the environment around your school. Or it can consist of helping other people in your community who are ill, elderly, hungry, lonely, or homeless. Such help, willingly and graciously offered, can make a great deal of difference to the lives of others.
- Research what is currently being done, and by whom, to address the problem or issue you have chosen. For example, if banning landmines is something of interest to you, there are numerous youth organizations already engaged in this effort that you might join. In addition to Mines Action Canada Youth, there is Young People for a Mine-Free World, which was started by the Youth Mine Action Ambassador Program (YMAAP) with the Red Cross, and the Mine Action Team of the Foreign Affairs Department of Canada.
- Figure out what organization or what area of need would best be served by your skills, abilities, and interests.
- Make more people aware of a problem using as many media forms as you can access. For example:
  - create a sign advertising a campaign to raise money for a good cause
  - write a letter to an editor of a newspaper that can be read by thousands of people in a single day if it is published
  - help organize a community meeting or a school assembly
  - make announcements over your school's PA system
  - hold a bake sale or car wash to raise money for a cause
  - create a web site
  - call into a radio talk show (local or CBC Cross Canada Checkup)

Consider starting a neighbourhood improvement program in your community.

Daniel Igali

CITIZEN IN ACTION

Daniel Igali

Daniel Igali was born in Nigeria, and entered Canada in 1994 when he applied for refugee status. He gained fame as a world-class wrestler and captured the hearts of Canadians when he won gold representing Canada in the 2000 Olympics. He displayed his joy and pride in being Canadian by kissing the flag and running joyfully in victory. In 2002, he demonstrated himself as a global citizen by returning to Nigeria and working to build a school. He raised money in Canada to build the school, which opened in 2006. Young people across Canada joined Daniel Igali's cause, including Ryan Hreljac of Ontario, who raised the money needed to build a water supply system that is the only source of clean drinking water for kilometres around the school.

What future impact might Daniel Igali's efforts to build a school in his native Nigeria have? Think in terms of the students who have the opportunity to attend that school.

APPLY YOUR LEARNING

1. You have read what Gandhi and others have said about citizen participation in democracy. Write your own statement, perhaps one or two sentences in length, expressing why you believe a citizen should participate in making change.
2. Sometimes, the obstacles to education some children face are not limited to a lack of school supplies. They are about things we take for granted, such as access to clean water and shelter from the elements. Read the following quotation:

   "For six years, my school has been a railroad car. It is difficult to learn. There is no glass in the windows. During summer it's impossible to stay cool, and during winter it's impossible to stay warm. During winter I wear all of my clothes: two pairs of pants, a shirt, a jacket and a hat. I don't have any gloves, so it's terrible to write. After one or two lessons in the cold, the teachers usually let us leave."
   — *Isa, a 17-year-old from Azerbaijan*

   What action(s) have you taken or could you take to contribute to the education of children in other parts of the world?

The Well-Rounded Citizen

ACTIVATE YOUR THINKING

Reflect on what you have learned in this book about having a citizenship focus. Record your thoughts in your journal.

Passport to Civics

Being a well-rounded citizen means being informed, having a purpose, and taking action.

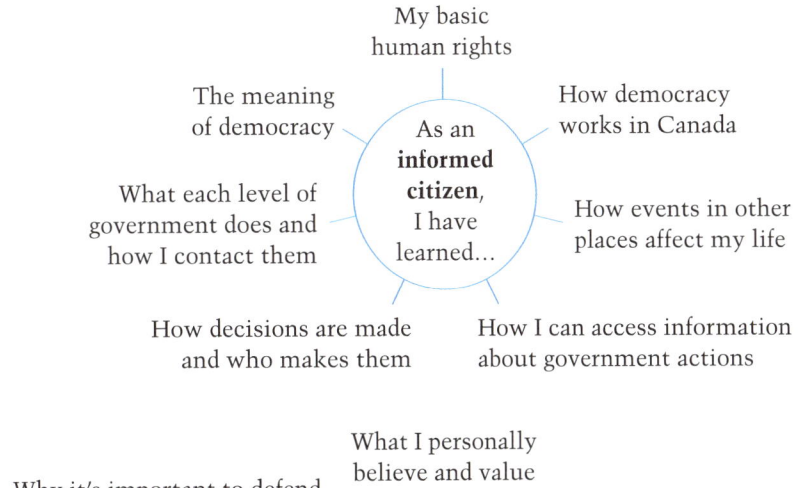

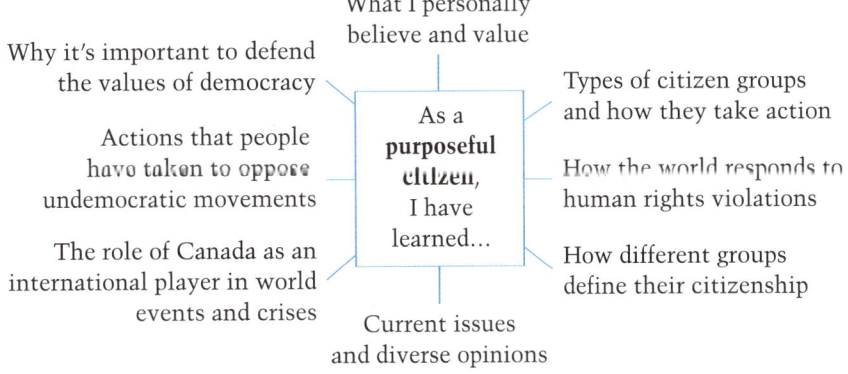

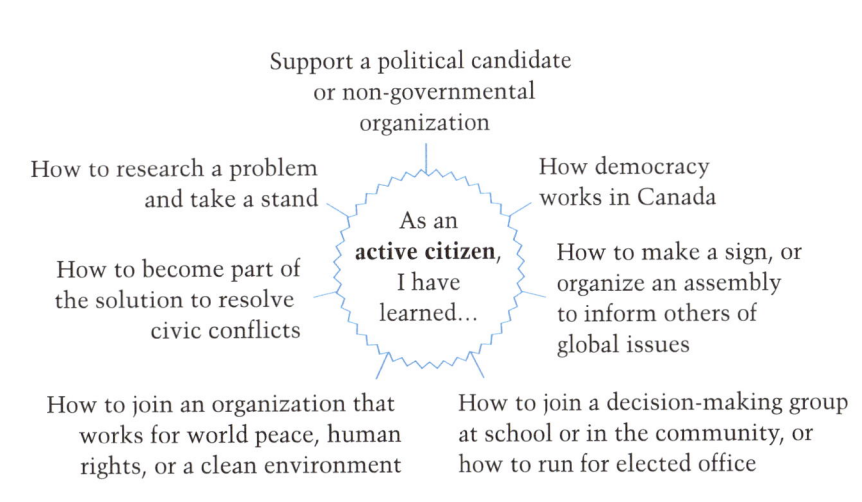

As an informed citizen, I have learned...
- My basic human rights
- How democracy works in Canada
- How events in other places affect my life
- How I can access information about government actions
- How decisions are made and who makes them
- What each level of government does and how I contact them
- The meaning of democracy

As a purposeful citizen, I have learned...
- What I personally believe and value
- Types of citizen groups and how they take action
- How the world responds to human rights violations
- How different groups define their citizenship
- Current issues and diverse opinions
- The role of Canada as an international player in world events and crises
- Actions that people have taken to oppose undemocratic movements
- Why it's important to defend the values of democracy

As an active citizen, I have learned...
- Support a political candidate or non-governmental organization
- How democracy works in Canada
- How to make a sign, or organize an assembly to inform others of global issues
- How to join a decision-making group at school or in the community, or how to run for elected office
- How to join an organization that works for world peace, human rights, or a clean environment
- How to become part of the solution to resolve civic conflicts
- How to research a problem and take a stand

APPLY YOUR LEARNING

1. In what other ways have you become a more informed, purposeful, and active citizen in addition to the ways listed above?
2. Create a collage that demonstrates your understanding of a well-rounded citizen. Post your collage in the classroom.

Global Citizenship

CHAPTER 5 REVIEW

Build Vocabulary and Understanding

1. Create a definition for each of the following words. Underline the *one* word in each definition that helps you understand the word best. Be sure the words are included in your personal dictionary.
    a) global village
    b) dictatorship
    c) diplomatic
    d) boycott
    e) theocratic
    f) genocide
    g) exterminate
    h) humanitarian
    i) tsunami
    j) landmines
    k) non-governmental organization
    l) refugee
    m) conscript

2. Explain in your own words what a global citizen is and why it is important to be one. Add a visual image to your definition, and share your work with the class. You might, for example, create a poster that would convince others of the importance of being a global citizen in the world today.

3. Write three questions that will help other students understand the main ideas of this chapter, and then prepare the possible answers. Try to have at least one question that can have more than one answer (called an open-ended question).

Think It Through

4. Research what is happening in Rwanda today.
    a) On one side of a T-chart, identify how citizens in Rwanda have responded to the human rights violations that took place.
    b) On the other side of the T-chart, describe how global citizens have responded to the human rights violations that took place.

Share Your Voice

5. a) Research the criteria for winning a Pearson Peace Medal.
   b) Write a letter nominating someone you have learned about in this book, or a person of your choice, for the prize. Provide evidence in your letter of the person's actions with respect to being a global citizen.

6. Create a visual collage for one of the following issues, and explain your choice of images to the class. Include a title that asks a question and provides a focus for your topic.
    - child soldiers
    - genocide
    - dictatorship
    - human rights
    - global citizen
    - your choice

7. Write a letter to the editor of a newspaper in which you explain your position on the actions of any authoritarian state that restricts human rights. Suggest what you believe all Canadian citizens can do to combat such governments.

Show You Care

8. a) Select any of the issues presented in this chapter. Create a web diagram of words, symbols, and pictures that explains what impact the issue is having on you. Use only one colour of ink for this task.
   b) Using a different colour of ink, update your web diagram with words, symbols, and pictures that explain what impact you are having on the issue.

Take Action Portfolio

9. Prepare your final presentation on what you did to make change. Use the following checklist to help guide you.
   a) State your issue and why you chose it.
   b) Provide some brief background information for others who may not be aware of the issue.
   c) Explain the action you took and include evidence (petition, poster, letter, signed log of volunteer hours spent, etc.).
   d) Evaluate the success of your action plan. In what ways was it successful? What changes took place as a result?
   e) Describe what you learned about yourself and about making a difference.
   f) List your future plans (next steps) on this or other issues.

Afterword

Congratulations! You can now consider yourself an informed, purposeful, and active citizen. You will be amazed at all that you will be able to accomplish when you dedicate yourself to making a difference. Work with others, and you will accomplish even more. Age, gender, race, and income do not matter—what is important is that you take action.

As you go forward on your journey, stay informed about the issues being debated in your school, your community, your country, and in the world at large. Remember to reflect on what you have already achieved, what strategies you used that were successful in the past, and thoughtfully consider what you can accomplish to bring about positive change. These are the first steps to becoming active and purposeful.

You may recall that a passport is one right of citizenship in a democratic nation. With the successful completion of this course you have truly earned your Passport to Civics.

Glossary

Aboriginal peoples: a term used in a general way to refer to First Nations peoples, Métis, and Inuit. *First Nations* refers to the original inhabitants of what is now Canada.

apartheid: an official policy that denies certain groups political, legal, and economic equality, keeping people separated based on racial or cultural differences

appellate court: a higher court that has the power to review and overturn the decision made by a lower court

arbitration: a process of resolving disputes in which the parties involved refer their problem to a knowledgeable, independent third party (an arbitrator) and agree in advance to accept the arbitrator's decision

authoritarian: a system of government in which rulers expect complete obedience from those they rule

citizen: a person who is a member of a particular country, and who has rights either because of being born there or because of having acquired citizenship to that country through immigration or through marriage

citizenship: the rights, duties, and responsibilities of a member of a state or nation

civics: the study of the rights and duties of citizenship

coalition government: a government consisting of two or more political parties, neither of which has a clear majority of the seats in parliament. These parties unite to form the government, dividing the cabinet positions between them.

common good: the interests of all people in a democratic society

constitution: a set of rules and practices by which a country is run

constitutional monarchy: powers of the monarch are limited by the nation's constitution and laws

culture: the beliefs, languages, customs, art, institutions characteristic of a particular community, people, or nation

democracy: a form of government in which all people have equal political power and input

direct democracy: a form of government in which decisions are made by a direct vote of the citizens

environment: the quality of the air, water and land in or on which people, animals and plants live

federal system: governmental power is divided between one central authority and several regional authorities

genocide: the systematic destruction of a nation, or an ethnic or religious group

***habeas corpus*:** an order requiring that a prisoner appear before a court to decide if his or her detention is lawful; protects against illegal imprisonment; from the Latin meaning "you have the body"

House of Commons (parliament): place where elected members of parliament (MPs) meet to discuss, debate, and vote on laws that the government wants to pass

indirect (representative) democracy: a form of government in which citizens elect representatives to make decisions on their behalf

interest groups: organizations that try to influence the government to make changes in laws or policies that will benefit their members or support a specific cause

judge: the person who is in charge of a trial in a court, and who decides how a person who is found guilty should be punished

judicial: anything relating to a court or system of law

jury: a group of people chosen from the community who hear the facts of a case and decide on the guilt or innocence of the accused

justice: the system for putting the law into action; the justice system

majority government: when one party has enough members in the House of Commons to outnumber the members of all other parties

massacre: the merciless killing of large numbers of innocent people

mediation: a process of resolving disputes in which an independent third party helps two or more parties work toward a solution that is acceptable to all parties

minority government: when the governing party controls fewer seats in the House of Commons than all other parties combined and must rely on MPs from other parties to support its legislation

monarchy: rule by a king or queen

North Atlantic Treaty Organization (NATO): a group of 26 countries from North America and Europe committed to safeguarding the freedom and security of member countries by political and military methods

political parties: voluntary associations of citizens who hold similar beliefs, values, and ideas on issues related to government

power: the ability to make things happen

prorogue: to discontinue parliament without formally ending the session

question period: part of the day during the sitting of the House of Commons (or legislative assembly at the provincial level) when opposition members can ask the government questions

republic: a political system where the supreme power rests with the voting public who elect representatives to the government. A republic is usually governed by these elected representatives and a president, but is not necessarily a democratic system of government

responsible government: a government that is accountable to its citizens through elected representatives

rule of law: everyone, no matter who they are, is subject to the same laws

Senate: forms the legislative branch of government, along with parliament; consists of appointed representatives who review and approve or request changes to laws proposed by parliament

throne speech: a speech written by the governing party, which outlines their plans for leading the government

values: personal or societal principles that govern a person's behaviour and choices

vote of non-confidence: a successful vote of non-confidence forces the government to resign and an election to be called. If a government budget or proposed law having to do with spending or raising money is ever defeated, it is considered a vote of non-confidence.

Index

A

Aboriginal peoples, 9, 44, 47, 55, 56, 66, 73, 95, 96, 97, 98, 100, 102, 107
Aboriginal place names, 107
Aboriginal rights, 34–35, 54–55, 66, 95–101, 114
Aboriginal self-government, 100–101
acronyms, 10, 115
Adams Mine, 106–107
Afghanistan, 10, 17, 19, 134, 136
AIDS, 81, 121, 123, 132
air pollution, 103–105
Amnesty International, 114, 118
Amnesty International Canada, 114, 115
Annan, Kofi, 122
anti-Semitism, 66–67
apartheid, 60
Arar, Maher, 64
arbitration, 63
Arbour, Louise, 128
armed forces. *See* soldiers
Asia, Southeast, 130–131
Assembly of First Nations, 48, 56
authoritarian decision-making, 7, 10–12
authoritarian rule, 10, 11–12, 60, 69, 116, 117–119, 127
autobiographies, 44, 79

B

ballots, 35–36, 37
Barnes, Kofi N., 61
Bartleman, James, 44, 56
Beaucage, John, 100–101
beliefs, 2, 8, 9, 14–17, 31, 32, 55, 56, 59, 64–65, 87, 95, 96, 115, 128, 139
bias, 61, 68
bilingualism, 9, 53
bills, 30, 42–43, 45
biographies, 79
Blackstock, Cindy, 73

Bloc Québécois, 9, 32, 36, 39
boycotts, 20, 79, 128
brainstorming, 8
British North America Act, 25, 53, 58
bullying, 68
by-laws, 45, 46, 92

C

cabinet ministers, 26, 28, 29, 30, 40, 42, 43, 46, 70–71
Caledonia, 98–99, 100
Canadian Charter of Rights and Freedoms, 53, 54–58, 61, 64–65, 66, 78, 96, 114, 115
Canadian Civil Liberties Association, 68, 88
Carella, Tony, 78–79
cartoons, 3, 44, 104
Cavoukian, Ann, 69–70
censorship, 88, 115
charities, 90, 91, 133, 136
charts, 2, 6, 67, 72
child labour, 124, 126
child rights, 123–124, 125, 128
child quality of life, 121–122, 125, 126
child soldiers, 123–126
citizen participation, 6, 18–20, 27–28, 32, 44, 46, 62, 76, 80–81, 90–92, 94, 95, 135, 137, 139
citizenship
   ceremony, 13, 14
   definition of, 2, 112, 139
   oath of, 14
   qualifications for, 12, 65
   rights and responsibilities of, 2, 7, 8, 12, 20, 37, 51–81, 90, 104–105, 127
   test, 12, 13, 14
   See also global citizenship
civics, 2, 8, 36
civil rights, 58, 67, 88, 112, 128
civil service, 28, 29, 92
civil war, 118, 119, 120, 128
coalition, 40

common good, 9, 10, 11, 12
community
   decision-making, 6–7, 139
   groups, 20, 45, 68, 73, 92
   improvement, 20, 68, 70, 91, 93–94, 97, 136, 137
   interests, 42, 78, 79, 92, 97
   problems, 72, 73, 75, 95, 106, 125, 128
conflict
   causes of, 86–89
   civic, 92, 94–101, 139
   environmental, 102–107
   ethnic, 120
   military, 16, 86, 112, 124, 125, 132, 136
conflict resolution, 62–63, 86, 87, 89–93, 96, 98–99, 100, 101, 107, 112, 127
   See also arbitration; mediation; negotiation
Conservative Party of Canada, 10, 31, 32, 36, 39
constitution, 11, 24, 53–54, 58, 60, 65, 66, 117, 118–119, 123
Constitution Act, 53, 55
councillors, 6, 7, 26, 45, 78–79
courts, 28, 29, 61–63, 65, 66–67, 73, 74, 121, 128, 129
crimes, 26, 66, 67–68, 72–76, 79–80, 95 120, 121, 128, 129
Criminal Code, 66, 67, 74
criminal law, 56–57, 72–74
Cukier, Wendy, 80
culture, 9, 15, 55, 56, 60, 68, 77, 78, 87, 96, 100, 112, 119, 128

D

Dallaire, Romeo, 120
death camps, 66, 67
debates, 33, 34, 35, 43, 45, 80, 101, 107
decision-making
   authoritarian, 7, 10–12
   consequences of, 2–3, 4, 8–9, 10, 11
   democratic, 7, 8–10, 11, 12, 15, 23, 90
   influences on, 28, 35, 46, 47, 95, 103
   levels of, 2–4
   judicial, 57, 61, 62, 63, 68
   methods of, 35, 40, 139
   organizational, 4, 5
   power in, 4–7, 12, 24, 47, 139

democratic decision-making, 7, 8–10, 11, 12, 15, 23, 90
democracy
   defined, 8, 23, 112, 139
   direct, 8
   features of, 12, 31, 32, 37, 39, 53, 59, 60, 69, 89, 116, 135, 139
   indirect, 8
   rights of, 55, 62, 70, 71, 79, 90
   values of, 14–17, 139
Denton, Dr. Richard, 106–107
Deseronto, 99, 100
dictatorships, 29, 114, 116
Direct Relief International, 135
disabled persons, 15, 36, 44, 54, 57, 64, 66, 114
Disaster Assistance Response Team (DART), 130–131, 133
disaster relief, 130–136
disasters, 127, 130–134, 136
discrimination, 55, 57, 60, 64, 65, 66–67, 77, 78, 124
   See also anti-Semitism; apartheid
diversity, 1, 9, 29, 54, 68
Doctors Without Borders, 136
Dyer, Corporal Ainsworth, 19

E

earthquakes, 130, 133–134, 135
education rights, 55, 58, 60, 112, 114, 124, 125
elections
   campaigns, 33–34, 46
   federal, 7, 30, 32, 33, 34, 35, 36–37, 38, 39, 40
   municipal, 7, 32, 33, 94, 107
   process, 30, 32, 33, 34, 35–36
   provincial/territorial, 7, 32, 33, 34, 37, 38, 40
   See also ridings; voting
Elections Canada, 32, 34, 37
Elections Ontario, 32, 34
Elizabeth II, Queen, 14, 53
Engineers Without Borders, 136
environmental protection, 77, 78, 79, 87, 88, 93, 100, 102, 104–107, 134, 137, 139
   See also waste management
equality rights, 15, 54, 55, 60, 64, 75, 123

F

families, 5, 68, 73, 77, 95, 121–122, 124, 125
Fathers of Confederation, 24
federal government
    branches of, 28–29, 61
    conflicts with, 87, 89, 90, 94–95, 96, 99, 100–101
    decision-making in, 10, 15, 24, 28, 35, 40, 90, 95
    law-making by, 15, 24, 34, 54, 58, 62
    powers and responsibilities of, 24–26, 41–43, 58, 61, 64, 69, 80, 102, 104, 130–131, 133, 139
    structure of, 28–29
flow charts, 42
Free the Children, 126
Freedom of Information and Protection of Privacy Act, 69, 70, 71
freedom of expression, 15, 55, 59, 66–67, 88, 113, 115, 117
    of information, 70, 71
    of peaceful assembly, 55, 59
    of religion, 15, 55, 113, 128
    protection of, 10, 16, 57, 78, 112, 113
    restrictions on, 58, 87, 88, 115, 116, 117, 128
fundraising, 16, 47, 79, 90, 91, 115, 137, 138

G

garbage. *See* waste management
gender violence, 79–81
genocide, 66, 67, 112, 120–122, 129
George, Anthony (Dudley), 98
global citizenship, 111–139
global village, 112, 127
Goddard, Captain Nichola, 19
governor general, 28, 29–30, 33, 39, 42, 43
graphs, 67
Green Party of Canada, 32, 36
gun control, 80
gun crimes, 26, 76, 79–80

H

habeas corpus, 57
Harper, Rt. Hon. Stephen, 10, 26, 31, 39, 64

hate crimes, 67–68, 88, 120
heroism, 3–4, 16–17, 19, 29, 79, 103
Holland, Mark, 35, 42
Holocaust, 66, 67, 112, 120
House of Commons, 9, 28, 29, 30, 39, 40, 42, 43, 46
humanitarian aid, 114, 121–123, 127, 130–135
Humphrey, John Peters, 54, 114
hurricanes, 130, 132–133
Hussein, Saddam, 11–12

I

idiomatic language, 90
Igali, Daniel, 138
Ignatieff, Michael, 40
immigrants, 9, 20, 29, 65, 132
In Flanders Fields, 17
information
    access to, 69, 70–71, 139
    protection of, 68, 69–70, 71
Information and Privacy Commissioner (IPC), 69–70, 71
interest groups, 42, 46, 47, 73, 92, 102–103, 128
International Criminal Court, 129
International Criminal Tribunal, 121
International Federation of Red Cross and Red Crescent Societies, 131–132
international treaties, 125–126, 129, 134
Internet, 23, 68, 69, 91, 112, 137
internment camps, 65
Inuit Circumpolar Council, 100
Ipperwash, 98, 99, 100
Iran, 116–118
Iraq, 11-12, 127, 129, 136

J

Jackson, Simon, 102–103
Jean, Rt. Hon. Michaëlle, 29, 33
Jubran, Azmi, 68
judges, 28, 29, 30, 45, 59, 60, 61–63, 74
judicial system, 59–60, 61–63, 65, 72–76, 117, 118, 121, 128, 129
juries, 61–62, 74

K

Kazemi, Zahra, 118
Keegstra, James, 66–67
Kielburger, Craig, 126
King, Martin Luther, Jr., 67
Kirsch, Philippe, 129
Korea, North, 116, 127–128

L

L'Arche, 15
land rights, 95–100
landmines, 128–129, 137
land-use agreements, 102
language rights, 54, 55, 57, 58, 119
law-making, 41–43, 45–46
leadership, 19, 31, 32, 33, 34, 37–40, 48, 97, 122, 123, 126, 128, 129, 131
legal rights, 55, 56–59, 60, 62
Léger, Cardinal Paul-Émile, 114
legislative members, 8, 33, 38, 39, 40, 43, 45, 46, 122
letter writing, 27–28, 46, 71, 79, 102, 115, 137
Lewis, Stephen, 122–123
Liberal Party of Canada, 9, 32, 33, 35, 36, 39, 40, 42
lieutenant governors, 29, 33, 43, 44, 56
lobbying, 46–48, 80, 125
Lobbyists' Code of Conduct, 47
logos, 32, 113
Lu, Bill, 20

M

Macdonald, Rt. Hon. Sir John A., 24
Machel, Graça, 125
Magna Carta, 59
Magnaville, 132–133
majority, 9, 12, 33, 38, 40, 118, 120
Mandela, Nelson, 60
Martin, Rt. Hon. Paul, 33, 39, 130
mayors, 6, 26, 33, 45, 66, 75, 106, 107
McCrae, John, 17
McGuinty, Dalton, 26, 99
McLachlin, Beverley, 62

McLuhan, Marshall, 112
Médecins Sans Frontières, 136
media, 40, 47–48, 112, 132, 137
mediation, 63
Members of Parliament (MPs), 10, 28, 33, 35, 38, 40, 42, 43, 46, 47
Members of Provincial Parliament (MPPs). *See* legislative members
Mewhinney, Richard, 93–94
Miller, David, 26, 75, 107
mind maps, 4
minority, 9, 12, 38–39, 40, 118, 120
minority rights, 55, 58, 64, 114
monarchy, 11, 14, 28, 29, 30, 53, 59–60, 95, 116
Mugabe, Robert, 118–119
municipal governments
    conflicts with, 87, 89, 90, 94–95
    decision-making in, 6–7, 90, 95
    law-making by, 45–46, 69, 71, 92
    power and responsibilities of, 25–26, 41, 78–79, 92, 139

N

negotiation, 127, 129
New Democratic Party of Canada, 9, 32, 36, 39, 45
New Democratic Party of Ontario, 122
newspaper articles, 9, 36, 63
Nigeria, 114–115, 138
Nobel Peace Prize, 60, 128, 136
non-governmental organizations, 134–135, 139
non-profit organizations, 91
North Atlantic Treaty Organization (NATO), 10, 19
notwithstanding clause, 58
Nunavut, 101

O

Oka crisis, 96–97, 98, 99, 100
Onley, David, 44
opinions. *See* point of view
opposition, 10, 11, 60, 87, 107, 116, 117, 128, 139
opposition parties, 38, 39–40, 118, 122
organizational chart, 6
OXFAM, 134–135

P

Pakistan, 130, 133–134, 135
paragraph composition, 20
Parliament, 28, 29, 30, 33, 38, 39, 40, 60
peace, 16, 60, 113, 114, 120, 122, 128, 136, 139
peacekeeping, 16, 19, 120–121, 127
Pearson Peace Medal, 114, 122
PEN Canada, 115
Persons Case, 65
persuasive language, 127
petitions, 28, 46, 79, 115
plebiscites, 101
point of view, 27, 30, 32, 35, 36, 40, 42, 46, 47, 55, 77, 86–88, 90, 91, 115, 117, 129, 139
political parties, 28, 30, 31, 32, 33, 37–38, 39–40, 46, 118, 122
polling stations, 35–36
poppy, 16, 17
power, 4
    abuse of, 116, 117, 118–119, 120, 128
    in decision-making, 4–7, 12, 24, 47, 103, 139
    of government, 24–26, 37, 38, 53, 58, 59–60, 61, 65, 116
premiers, 26, 29, 33, 37, 43, 48, 93, 98, 99, 102
pressure groups. *See* interest groups
prime ministers, 10, 16, 24, 26, 28, 29, 30, 31, 33, 37, 39, 40, 53, 64, 130
privacy rights, 68–69, 70–71
private members' bills, 42, 45
protests, 55, 79, 86, 87, 96, 98, 99, 107, 115
provincial/territorial governments
    conflicts with, 87, 89, 90, 93, 94–95, 98–99
    decision-making in, 5, 24, 40, 90, 95
    law-making by, 43, 54, 58, 66, 69, 71, 106, 107
    powers and responsibilities of, 24–26, 41, 61, 104, 131, 139
public awareness campaigns, 16, 44, 104, 115, 125, 136, 137
public inquiries, 45, 98
public service announcements, 68, 103

Q

question period, 40

R

Red Cross, 121, 130, 137
refugees, 133–134, 138
Remembrance Day, 16, 17, 30
republic, 116
responsible government, 53
restorative justice, 73
ridings, 33, 34, 36, 37, 38
rights
    Aboriginal, 34–35, 54–55, 66, 95–101, 114
    civil, 58, 67, 88, 112, 128
    education, 55, 58, 60, 112, 114, 124, 125
    equality, 15, 54, 55, 60, 64, 75, 123
    language, 54, 55, 57, 58, 119
    legal, 55, 56–59, 60, 62, 73
    minority, 42, 55, 58, 64, 114
    privacy, 68–69
    treaty, 55, 96, 98, 100
rights violations, 64–68, 71, 81, 86, 114, 116–127, 128, 139
rule of law, 59–60
Rwanda, 119–123, 128

S

Saro-Wiwa, Ken, 114–115
schools, 5, 6, 68, 115, 131, 133, 138, 139
Senate, 28, 29, 30, 39, 42, 43, 65
signs, 106, 137, 139
soldiers, 10, 17, 19, 96, 98, 120–121
    See also child soldiers; peacekeeping
Spirit Bear Coalition, The, 102–103
Stop the Violence, 76
Stronach, Frank, 132–133
Student Votes, 36, 37
Supreme Court of Canada, 28, 29, 61–62, 65, 66–67
surveys, 30, 67
symbols, 106

T

Tax Court of Canada, 61
throne speech, 30
treaty rights, 55, 96, 98, 100
trials, 57, 60, 74, 117, 118, 121

Index 149

Trudeau, Rt. Hon. Pierre, 53
tsunamis, 130–131

U

UNICEF, 122, 134
United Nations, 88, 100, 112–116, 120–121, 122, 123, 125, 128, 129, 133–134
United States, 11, 19, 24, 127–128, 129, 130, 132–133
Universal Declaration of Human Rights, 54, 112–116

V

values, 2, 3, 8, 14–17, 31, 32, 54, 56, 57, 64–65, 67, 87, 95, 115, 139
Vanier, Jean, 15
Venn diagrams, 11
veterans, 16–17
violence, 10, 11, 74, 75, 76, 98, 120, 124
    See also gender violence
volunteer service, 15, 46, 73, 78, 90–91, 93–94, 126, 131, 133, 134, 135, 137
vote of non-confidence, 39
voter apathy, 36–37, 94
voters' list, 34–35
voting, 7, 9, 15, 28, 37, 46, 77, 79
    See also elections

voting age, 34, 35, 36, 42
voting rights, 60, 66, 97, 116, 117, 118–119

W

war crimes, 67, 128
waste management, 105–107, 137
White Ribbon Movement, 80, 81
Wiesenthal, Simon, 67
Williams, Jody, 128–129
Winters, Chuck, 76
Wiwa, Ken, 115
women, 65, 79–81, 123
word building, 112
World War I, 16, 131
World War II, 16, 65, 66, 67, 98, 112, 120, 134
wrongful detention, 115, 117, 128

Y

Youth Criminal Justice Act, 72, 73–74
youth activism, 125, 126, 137, 138
youth justice, 72–76

Z

Zimbabwe, 116, 118–119

Acknowledgements

Every effort has been made to identify and credit sources. Please inform Pippin Publishing of any omissions.

/9 CBC.ca-Reprinted with permission /10 CBC.ca-Reprinted with permission /20 Torstar Syndication Services-Reprinted with permission /26 CBC.ca-Reprinted with permission /39 CTV.ca-Reprinted with permission /46 City of Waterloo By-Law No. 91-101. Reprinted with permission /93 Press release from the Office of the Premier of Nova Scotia, August 29, 2005. Reprinted with permission /99 Canadian Press-Reprinted with permission /100 Excerpted, with permission, from a Union of Ontario Indians media release, July 21, 2005 /102 Excerpted, with permission, from www.spiritbearyouth.org /134 voanews.com /136 Excerpted, with permission, from the Engineers Without Borders 2004 Annual Report

Photo Credits

Photographs are listed in order of their appearance on the page, left to right, top to bottom.

/1 Getty Images /4 CoolClips.com /5 Shutterstock; *Toronto Star*-Vince Talotta /6 Evergreen, Courtesy of Town of Richmond Hill /12 www.dfait-maeci.gc.ca/Canada-magazine/issue29/07-title-en.asp, Department of Foreign Affairs and International Trade, 2006. Reproduced with the permission of Her Majesty the Queen in Right of Canada, represented by the Minister of Foreign Affairs, 2006 /13 www.gg.ca/media/pho/index_e.asp?GalleryID=338&Sequence=3, Office of the Secretary to the Governor General of Canada, 2007, MCpl Issa Paré, Rideau Hall, July 1, 2007. Reproduced with the permission of the Minister of Public Works and Government Services, 2007 /15 L'Arche Canada; www.gg.ca/media/pho/index_e.asp?GalleryID=357&Sequence=3, Office of the Secretary to the Governor General of Canada, 2007, Sgt Éric Jolin, Rideau Hall, June 19, 2007. Reproduced with the permission of the Minister of Public Works and Government Services, 2007 /16 Reproduced with the permission of Veterans Affairs Canada, 2007; Reproduced with the permission of Veterans Affairs Canada, 2006 /17 Cameron Bevers; The Poppy image is used with the permission of The Royal Canadian Legion /18 Courtesy of University of Guelph; Courtesy of Canadian Alliance for Development Initiatives and Projects (Cadip) /19 Source: Corporal Ainsworth Dyer, 1977-2002. http://www.army.forces.gc.ca/lfwa_hq/Eulogies_Dyer.htm. Department of National Defence. Reproduced with the permission of the Minister of Public Works and Government Services Canada, 2006; Source: Captain Nichola Goddard. http://www.army.gc.ca/lf/English/6_1_1.asp?FlashEnabled=1&id=1048. Department of National Defence. Reproduced with the permission of the Minister of Public Works and Government Services Canada, 2006 /20 *Toronto Star*-Ron Bull /21 Shutterstock /23 Cartoon by Pat Cupples /24 CP-Steve White; Library and Archives Canada/C-001855 /26 Source: Tackling Crime Through Bail Reform (Image 20061123_PM_feature_BailReform.jpg). Year of publication: Nov. 23, 2006. Reproduced with the permission of the Minister of Public Works and Government Services, 2007, and Courtesy of the Privy Council Office; Courtesy of Association of Municipalities of Ontario (AMO) /29 Chart by Christopher Johnson; www.gg.ca/media/pho/index_e.asp?GalleryID=332&Sequence=9, Office of the Secretary to the Governor General of Canada, 2007, MCpl Issa Paré, Rideau Hall, June 15, 2007. Reproduced with the permission of the Minister of Public Works and Government Services, 2007 /31 www.gg.ca/media/pho/index_e.asp?GalleryID=200&Sequence=3, Office of the Secretary to the Governor General of Canada, 2006, Sgt Éric Jolin, Rideau Hall, February 6, 2006. Reproduced with the permission of the Minister of Public Works and Government Services, 2006 /32 Courtesy of Bloc Québécois; Courtesy of First Peoples National Party of Canada; Courtesy of Green Party of Canada; Courtesy of Canada's New Democratic Party; Courtesy of Marijuana Party; Courtesy of Libertarian Party of Canada; Courtesy of Liberal Party of Canada /33 http://gg.ca/media/pho/galleryPics/797.jpg, Office of the Secretary to the Governor General of Canada, 2007. Reproduced with the permission of the Minister of Public Works and Government Services, 2007; *Toronto Star*-Hans Deryk /34 Courtesy of Brandon University /35 Jean-Marc Carisse; Richard McGuire /36 Source: Elections Canada /37 Courtesy of Student Vote; www.CartoonStock.com /39 CP-Tom Hanson /40 Jean-Marc Carisse, courtesy of the Office of the Leader of the Opposition /42 Library of Parliament-Roy Grogan /43 Legislative

Assembly of Ontario /44 Philippe Landreville; Steve Nease /45 Courtesy of *Rainy River Record* /46 Courtesy of City of Waterloo; Courtesy of Lee Richardson /51 Shutterstock /52 iStock; Shutterstock /53 Robert Cooper, National Archives of Canada, Pierre Trudeau Photo Collection. Reprinted with permission /54 The Department of Canadian Heritage. Reproduced with the permission of the Minister of Public Works and Government Services Canada, 2006 /55 Ellen Rayner, Courtesy of OPSEU Local 659 /56 Indian and Northern Affairs Canada. Reproduced with the permission of the Minister of Public Works and Government Services, 2007; Courtesy, City of Toronto. Used with permission. All rights reserved. /57 Source: *Justice Canada*: A newsletter from the Department of Justice. www.justice.gc.ca/en/dept/pub/jc/vol2/no3/page5.html, Department of Justice, 2002. Reproduced with the permission of the Minister of Public Works and Government Services Canada, 2007 /59 Christian Peacemaker Teams; Sea Shepherd Conservation Society; Canadian Federation of Students – Ontario /60 Nelson Mandela Foundation-Matthew Willman /61 Source: *Justice at Work*: A recruitment magazine from the Department of Justice. www.canada.justice.gc.ca/en/dept/pub/recru, Department of Justice, 2006. Reproduced with the permission of the Minister of Public Works and Government Services Canada, 2007 /62 Cartoon by Pat Cupples; Supreme Court of Canada-Philippe Landreville; Source: Outline of Canada's Court System. www.justice.gc.ca/en/dept/pub/trib/page3.html, Department of Justice Canada, 2005. Reproduced with the permission of the Minister of Public Works and Government Services Canada, 2006. Adapted by Christopher Johnson /64 CP-Tom Hanson /65 Tak Toyota/Library and Archives Canada/C-046350 /66 Source: Library and Archives Canada/Department of Indian Affairs and Northern Development Collection/PA-203105, Department of Indian Affairs and Northern Development. Reproduced with the permission of the Minister of Public Works and Government Services Canada, 2007; United States Holocaust Memorial Museum /67 Jim Mendenhall, Courtesy of Simon Wiesenthal Center; Source: Statistics Canada: *The Daily*, Catalogue 11-001, Tuesday, June 1, 2004. Statistics Canada information is used with the permission of Statistics Canada. Users are forbidden to copy this material and/or redisseminate the data, in an original or modified form for commercial purposes, without the express written permission of Statistics Canada /68 Shutterstock /69 Office of the Information and Privacy Commissioner/Ontario /70 Office of the Information and Privacy Commissioner/Ontario /73 Congress of Aboriginal Peoples-Garrison Garrow; Courtesy of Cindy Blackstock /76 Courtesy of The Argos Foundation-Stop the Violence /79 Courtesy of City of Vaughan /81 Courtesy of The White Ribbon Campaign /85 Shutterstock /86 Courtesy of Steve Corbett /87 Courtesy of PETA /89 Shutterstock /91 Courtesy of Volunteer Canada /92 Nik Luka, courtesy of We Live Here /93 Reproduced with the permission of Communications Nova Scotia, 2007 /94 Courtesy of Richard Mewhinney; photograph by Virginia Milarchuk /95 Christian Peacemaker Teams /96 Christian Peacemaker Teams /97 CP-Ryan Remiorz; Map by Christopher Johnson /98 CP-Carolyn George /99 CP-Jonathan Hayward /100 Courtesy of The Inuit Circumpolar Council Canada; Courtesy of Union of Ontario Indians /101 Courtesy of Nunavut Legislative Assembly /102 Courtesy of Simon Jackson /103 Reprinted with permission granted by the Halton Partners for Clean Air, Halton Region and the City of Burlington; Source: Idling Gets You Nowhere (CPPI "Idling Gets You Nowhere" air fresheners). URL: http://oee.nrcan.gc.ca/transportation/idling/material/cppi-campaign.cfm?attr=28#air. Natural Resources Canada, 2006. Reproduced with the permission of the Minister of Public Works and Government Services Canada, 2006 /104 Published with permission from the City of Toronto /107 CP-Jim Rankin; CP-Jonathan Hayward /111 Map by Christopher Johnson /113 Reproduced with the permission of the United Nations /114 Ken Bell/Library and Archives Canada/PA-203443; Canada Post Corporation {1981}. Reproduced with permission /115 Courtesy of Amnesty International Canada; AP-*Sunday Alabama* /117 Map by Christopher Johnson /118 Map by Christopher Johnson /119 Map by Christopher Johnson /120 Courtesy of United States Holocaust Memorial Museum /121 Courtesy of United States Holocaust Memorial Museum /122 Médecins Sans Frontières (MSF), 2004, Courtesy of Stephen Lewis Foundation /124 UNICEF/HQ97-0179/Roger Lemoyne /125 CP-Fred Greenslade; AP-Kittinun Rodsupan /126 UNICEF/HQ01-0093/Stevie Mann; Courtesy of Free the Children /128 Arpan Munier, United Nations Mission in Sudan /129 Courtesy of Mines Action Canada; ICC-CPI/Wim Van Cappellen, ICC-CPI/Hans Hordijk /131 Source: IS2005-1032a, Ampara district, MCpl Paul MacGregor, Canadian Forces Combat Camera, National Defence, 2005. Reproduced with the permission of the Minister of Public Works and Government Services, 2008 /132 Reproduced with the permission of The International Federation of Red Cross and Red Crescent Societies; Source: HS2005-G002-04, Photo by MCpl Colin Kelley, Canadian Forces Combat Camera, National Defence. Reproduced with the permission of the Minister of Public Works and Government Services, 2006 /133 Courtesy of Magna International Inc.-Nick Persichilli; Map by Christopher Johnson /134 AP-Tomas Munita /135 Courtesy of Direct Relief International /136 Courtesy of Engineers Without Borders Canada /137 Courtesy of Volunteer Canada /138 Courtesy of Daniel Igali /142 Shutterstock